Yardie

Yardie

*Struggles of a Young Jamaican
growing up in New York
A MEMOIR*

David G Heron

To order additional copies of this book, contact:
Xlibris Corporation
1-888-795-4274
www.Xlibris.com
Orders@Xlibris.com
96135

In memory of Samuel and Madeline Heron, whose love has contributed to me in writing this book. If it wasn't for their love, I would probably be angry and afraid of life.

Thanks, Dad, for telling me to always hitch my wagon to a star, and, in your own way, expressed that you loved me—words that all little black boys need to hear from their fathers.

Mom, thanks for your patience, nurturing, and unconditional love. You have taught me how good it is to share, by your example of sharing so much with others. Thanks for starting me on my journey; your legacy lives on. I miss your smile.

Preface

I was inspired to write this book after taking a trip to Jamaica in July 2001. I am not one of those Jamaicans who always go home for a getaway and would've gone to some other island, if the spirit had led me. But I just had this inner urge to go there at this particular time and didn't know why. I told everyone I was going there to check the Victor Dixon High School of the Northern Caribbean University (formerly West Indies College), where I was considering sending my son, Michael, to and did visit there. I also told them that I felt very burnt-out from working two jobs in New York City and just needed to get away to recharge my batteries. However, these were all attempts to legitimize going because I truly didn't know why I needed to go. But once I arrived there, a series of incidents started occurring from the first night I got on the island that I knew I needed to start keeping a journal.

From around the third day I was there, I started to feel that these incidents were more than mere coincidences and suspected they were going to continue for the duration of my trip. Yes, to some, they may appear as just an adventure, but as you will find out, they were much more. For many years, I tried to make sense out of all that happened but could never find an explanation. I tried verbalizing some of my experiences to others only to realize it was very difficult to articulate. Until one day, it came to me that the answer and the question are somehow the same. In other words, my questions must be the answer. It wasn't meant for me to figure out; it was meant to just be and to experience what I experienced.

My journal evolved into this book after I held on to it for about six years and, one day, picked it up to read. I wasn't sure what I was going to do with it and thought I would just read through it and then throw it away. Anyway, as I began reading, I was immediately transported back in time to Jamaica. The more I read, the more vivid those experiences came back to me. The book's contents also include reflections of some of my childhood experiences growing up in Jamaica and New York.

I have tried to stay away from using conjectures in my writing and have even used the actual names of my characters as they were known. Please bear in mind though that many of these names were really a.k.a.'s. I used my journal to document specific occurrences that had happened in Jamaica, which allowed me to give a more accurate account of what I had experienced on this trip. Yet while I was transcribing the material from my journal, it brought back memories of the past that I also included in this memoir. Nothing was conjured up to make for more exciting reading, and to the best of my recollection, everything written in this book is gospel truth.

As hard as I try to make this a happy book, there are going to be some who are going to be offended by something I wrote. I apologize for this in advance and ask that you don't take it personally as it is only my subjective analysis on the subject or, if you prefer, "my spin on things." If you've reached a point where you are truly offended and just can't read any further, then I implore you before you go, to read the concluding chapters. This is assuming, of course, that the concluding chapters are not the source of your offense. Happy reading.

Acknowledgments

I want to give thanks to all the people who made it possible for me to write this book.

First, to my wife, Vadne, who allowed me to leave her alone with the boys while I ventured on my trip to Jamaica to have this experience.

I also give thanks to my brother, Barrie, who I remembered telling me at a very young age that I could grow up to be whatever I wanted.

Thanks to my good friend, Julian Brown, who I call genius because you're so brilliant. Thank you for your technical assistance and help on the computer. I know your passion, and I encourage you to write your own book. You already have all the materials.

To my nephews Noel and Andrew in Atlanta, who were two of the first people I told I was writing a book, and they would always ask me, "How is the book coming?" Thanks for revering me as your uncle; I always feel your love.

To Grace McGhee, my manager from the Visiting Nurse Service of New York. You are responsible for creating the best work experience I ever had, and I wish everybody could have a manager like you. You are phenomenal, and I meant it when I told you you're the best.

To Wayne Walters, time and distance can never diminish true friendship; you'll always be my best friend.

To my Aunt Ven in Birmingham, England, for naming the bambino after me. Thanks for the honor.

And to David, my namesake, thank you for telling me I am an inspiration to you. That's a big compliment.

Last but not least, special thanks to Karlon Cromwell, for giving me your time, suggestions, and ideas. Your help was invaluable.

The First Day

Jamaica was my home for the first fourteen years of my life. During the sixties, my father decided to migrate to the United States, and upon obtaining his green card and permanent resident status, he decided to send for my mother and me to join him in New York. I remembered that day very clearly on July 20, 1969, as it was the day man first set foot on the moon.

I decided to write this book after going back to Jamaica where I hadn't visited as an adult for several years. I had always gone back with family members (my mom and dad and / or wife and young kids), but this time, I wanted to go without them. I just felt a deep desire I couldn't resist and told my wife I was going to go there although I know she wouldn't like the idea.

My mom didn't want me to go to Jamaica either as it was common knowledge to everyone how violent the island had become, and she let me know she was very afraid for my safety. I was the youngest of her three children, and she would always tell me I was the closest to her heart. Geographically, I was also the closest as my brother and eldest sibling lived in Windsor, Canada, and my sister, who I followed, had left New York and moved to Miami.

I called up my cousin, Vaughn, a police detective working in Mandeville, who my mother loved and was always worried about him working as a policeman in Jamaica. He told me the violence everyone was talking about was confined to certain areas and that even if I was going through those areas, I didn't have anything to worry about as most of the violence were gang related. That's all I needed to hear and was enough information for me to start planning my trip.

I told my cousin, Diana, about my spur-of-the-moment decision to go to Jamaica. She is a nurse and flies down to Jamaica several times a year. She owns a house in Christiana, a small town located about ten miles north of Mandeville and has an apartment in Kingston, where her older son, David, was attending high school and younger son, Rasheed, was in elementary school. Joan, her younger sister who is a teacher, took care of them, but she was practically in Jamaica every other weekend.

Diana told me she would fly down with me and that we could hang together in Jamaica. I was actually planning to stay with Aunt Tot, her mother, in the country and still planned on doing so. I wanted to get away from the hustle-bustle type of living in New York and looked forward to the peace and tranquility I expected to find up in the hills of Craig Head where my mother grew up and where Diana was born.

I had no doubt that the little respite I needed I could find in Craig Head, which is located up in the mountains just a couple miles further north of Christiana. This is the town area for people in Craig Head and surrounding villages such as Pike and Colyville, where everyone goes to the market to shop or sell what they grow in their fields. Christiana is mountainous in its own right, overlooking Trelawny, its neighboring parish.

Diana and I were more like soul mate cousins. We shared the same belief systems about politics and religion and life in general. I really loved and respected her and also admired her accomplishments as a no-nonsense person, a businesswoman,

and a single mother. I started my journey back to Jamaica
with Diana after leaving New York City's John F. Kennedy
International Airport not knowing what to expect, only feeling
deep inside that this was not going to be just a trip to Jamaica,
but a journey that I would somehow never forget.

*   *   *

Diana and I talked all the way until we reached Montego Bay
Airport, which made the flight seem shorter. I had to throw away
some organic Gala apples at the airport because customs would
not let me bring them into the country. I was going to eat them
on the plane, but I was just too busy conversing with Diana and
forgot. I was kind of concerned about how I would eat in Jamaica
being a vegetarian and knowing that Diana was not.

Vegetarianism was one of the topics we discussed on the plane. She
told me about a research that was conducted about certain blood
types that couldn't support a vegetarian diet. She explained how the
author was always sick and weak after becoming a vegetarian and
how the author discovered it was directly related to his blood type.
I got the feeling she was really trying to explain to me her reason for
being a meat eater, and I told her I would check out the research
and the book the author had written about his findings.

Vaughn was waiting for us at the airport in Montego Bay with
his girlfriend, Desrene, and their three-year-old son, Chad. He
was driving a black made-for-America Toyota Celica with the
steering wheel on the left. Most of the cars in Jamaica have right
steering wheels as in Jamaica, like the majority of British islands,
people drive on the left-hand side of the road. A few taxi drivers
outside the airport with larger vehicles came over, asking to take
us to our destination, thinking (like we were) that our luggage
wasn't going to fit in Vaughn's little Celica. However, he was
able to fit the luggage with a lot of prodding and used a piece
of rope to tie them down.

It rained on the way to Manchester. We went through Mandeville and passed by Cynthia's (our eldest cousin) home in Christiana before climbing the road going up the mountain into Craig Head. The view of the mountainside was nothing less than spectacular—it was breathtaking. The road was steep and spiral, overlooking Trelawny on the other side to the right. I had a flashback to when I was a little youngster in Jamaica, making the trip with my mother going up this same road.

Diana's dad, Papa (as he was called by everyone) was home alone when we got to the house up in Craig Head. He was downstairs in the shop that is located in the lower landing to the left side of the house. Customers could access the shop from outside by going through a gate and climbing down a flight of stairs from the road. Diana had built this house for her parents, which has several bedrooms, a bathroom and a kitchen on both levels to accommodate families traveling from abroad or from town (Kingston). Aside from local foods and general supplies, the shop also had a lot of foreign merchandise brought back from America by Diana on her frequent trips back home. Papa also brought back stuff to sell when he traveled to America. Aunt Tot was visiting Dimple in Washington, DC, at the time and would undoubtedly be bringing some stuff home to sell also.

*   *   *

The sun had set, and we soon got settled in after Vaughn had left. Papa gave us dinner, which consisted of yellow yams, green bananas, dumplings, and fish. The house was dim and didn't have hot water, so I had to brave it and take a well-needed shower in what felt like ice-cold water. After unpacking a little and changing my clothes, I joined Papa and Diana downstairs in the shop.

Diana was definitely in her element back home. Speaking in patois to Papa, she appeared to have returned in time as a little girl excited to see her daddy. The local vernacular made her sound real country and different from how I am accustomed to hearing her speak. I was listening to them very attentively when all of a sudden, everything went black. The light in the dimly lit shop was out, and everywhere was pitch-black. It was a blackout. Diana seemed to regain her bearings and said in proper English, "Welcome to Jamaica, Dave." Papa got his flashlight and went for the kerosene lamps next door inside the house. Diana assisted in lighting them and brought one upstairs. Papa closed the shop as the customer who had stopped by and had chatted with them for a little while left.

"Where is Everald?" Diana inquired to Papa. Everald was her nephew. He was around nine years old and the son of her estranged brother, Mikey. Mikey was sort of the black sheep of the family. When I was a little boy growing up in Maverley, a little village in St. Andrew, just outside Kingston, our grandmother, Sistah (sister), paid us a visit from the country and brought Mikey with her. We were very excited and happy to see them, but Mikey was the typical spoiled grandchild. I supposed we were playing a little too rough with him when he ran crying to Sistah. To our great surprise, she got very upset, told everyone good-bye, and left with Mikey still crying. There was no doubt she thought her Kingstonian grandchildren were just too "rude" (naughty). Mikey was now a crybaby to his cousins in Kingston and has now inherited the nickname Cry-cry for short. He was not a favorite sibling of Diana either. When I asked about him on the flight to Jamaica, she described him as irresponsible, illiterate, and a kleptomaniac who would steal anything that was not nailed down.

Papa was running out of kerosene oil and didn't have enough to refuel the lamps. We took an additional flashlight and proceeded to walk to another shop approximately a half mile down the road. There were no streetlights or landline telephone in Craig Head or any of the other villages up the hill from Christiana. Although it was very dark, we passed a lot of young people walking and socializing on the way. There were young men zipping by on bicycles, using the lights from their cell phones as a source of illumination to prevent us from running into them in the pitch darkness. I was glad we were able to make it to the shop up the street without being run over or falling off the mountainside.

The shopkeeper was at the door, busily pouring kerosene oil into the containers of the customers who had lined up at the door. I could tell this was a regular routine for both the shopkeeper and the customers alike. Everyone who came to the shop, whether to buy kerosene or groceries, stayed at the shop for a good while, socializing and chitchatting with the shopkeeper. Papa, Diana, and I sat on a small wooden bench adjacent to the shop's counter where the shopkeeper's wife was waiting and talking to a customer. Nobody was in any rush to get back home with the kerosene oil. Everyone knew each other, and I was introduced as Ms. Tot's nephew from America to curious shoppers as they came into the shop. On the way back to the house, I couldn't help but notice how bright the stars in the sky were. They were so close and so many they seemed to light up the sky. I noticed a cluster of twenty, thirty, fifty, or more stars and thought that must be the Milky Way.

We opened the gate to the driveway, and standing in a corner on the veranda was Everald, his small lanky features barely visible in the darkness.

"Everald, come yah bwoy! A weh yuh did deh?"

"Mi a tell yuh dis yah bwoy pickney, him wokliss juss like I'm puppa," Papa stated.

As he started to cry, Diana became furious and went ballistic on the young boy too.

"Wah yuh a cry 'bout? Yuh juss like Mikey, mi a tell yuh. An' mi hear seh yuh a tief too, but if yuh ever tief anyting fi mi, I bruck off yuh finga dem," she said in a rage with her eyes popping.

Diana is a Virgo with dark piercing eyes that seem to penetrate you when she looks at you. Diana's confrontation with Everald seemed to be escalating, and it was plain to me that she was projecting her anger toward her brother unto his young son. I thought I was about to witness a real old-time Jamaican beat down. I was surprised at Diana but mostly afraid for little Everald. She was right up on him, pointing her fingers on his face, and he was terrified and was crying. I had to do something fast to rescue him.

"Come on, Diana," I said in a challenging but calm manner trying not to escalate the situation any further. "He's just a little kid." This is difficult to write, and my emotions are getting the better of me as I remember this. No child is ever entitled to this type of abuse and to be told he is worthless.

I reflected on my own childhood in Jamaica and the abuse (both verbal and physical) I had experienced growing up there. Looking back, did I really deserve all those beatings and floggings with belts, whips, switches, or anything they could get their hands on? I was thumped, slapped, punched, and was even beaten with a piece of a garden hose with the intent, I suppose, that one day this was going to make me into a model citizen. I mean, it wasn't just my mother (Dad only beat me once that I can remember) but my big brother, teachers, and certain neighbors who felt they had the special authority to apply the rod of correction in helping mold my character. I also knew better than to go home and complain to my mother that Ms. Lucy gave me a whipping. That would certainly bring up the question, what did you do to deserve that whipping? since adults are always right and could cause me to get another whipping.

Papa and Evrald

I hate to listen to those people who like to explain how much they benefited from all those abuses they experienced from loved ones during their childhood, especially those church folks with their "spare the rod and spoil the child" philosophy. They don't consider it an abuse because it is sanctioned by the Bible, which gives them the justification to beat and abuse their children. Some of those people also believed slavery was justified because of another passage in the Bible that states, "Slaves, obey your masters." Personally, I know that I would have benefited much better with a lot more nurturing or a simple explanation as to why I was getting the heck beaten out of me from the people who said they loved and cared about me.

That type of corporal punishment was nothing less than child abuse. Violence perpetuated on the defenseless young children would land their parents in jail if it happened in the United States. The reason why countless other children and I were beaten so much is simply because our caregivers didn't know any better. It was passed down through generations straight from the slave master. In Dr. Joy Degruy Leary's book, *Post Traumatic Slave Syndrome*, she explained that most of the violence we perpetuate on one another is directly related to the physical abuse our forefathers experienced during slavery days. I wonder if this could, in someway, explain the tremendous amount of violence on the island of Jamaica and other slave colonies in the Caribbean.

The beat down didn't take place, and Everald ran downstairs while I was still confronting Diana. I don't believe she even cared how upset I was, and she was still feeling justified in her rage and the beating she would have inflicted on her nine-year-old nephew had I not been there. The young boy was wearing tattered clothing and was barefoot and, later, told me he had been eating mangoes throughout the day and wasn't feeling hungry. It was now very late, and the kerosene lamp flickered in the dimly lit room where he fell asleep on the bed next to Papa. I breathed a sigh of relief and thanked God for preventing what might have been a real horrid incident.

The house in Craighead

*   *   *

The Second Day

I slept upstairs in the front bedroom adjacent to the veranda and woke up as usual at 5:00 AM, which was 4:00 AM Jamaican time. Before getting up, I had intended to read one of the books I had brought with me, but instead, I just continued lying there, thinking about what had transpired on my first day on the island, particularly last night. I had a feeling this was not going to be like any other trip I had ever taken to Jamaica or anywhere before for that matter. Oh boy, how true that was; I discovered as the days started to unfold that this was only the beginning.

"Dave!" Diana called as she entered into the bedroom. It was just a few minutes past four o'clock local time. "Come. Let's go do some meditation," she said. I picked up my Bible, *Our Daily Bread*, and *Daily Word* magazines I had brought with me on my trip and followed her into the deck at the back of the house. This part of the house was on stilts and faced the mountains in the distance at the other end of the valley. Dawn was slowly breaking, and the golden sun was getting ready to burst open through the cyan sky, promising that life would soon begin to stir the moment it burst through. Soon, there would be women sweeping their yards or cooking breakfast in their outdoor kitchens and men scurrying off to work and children going to school.

The mineral-rich red ground was just flooded with all types of tropical vegetation: jackfruit, mango, banana, coconut trees, sugarcane, and yellow yam, to name a few. Cows and goats were grazing freely. A little further away, there were speckles of light in houses surrounding the hills and valley. I don't know why, but it reminded me of the poem "Daffodils" by William Wordsworth that I had to memorize in elementary school.

I wandered lonely as a cloud / that floats on high o'er vales and hills / when all at once I saw a crowd / a host, of golden daffodils.

Except there weren't any daffodils that I saw.

We did some stretching and deep breathing before sitting down on the two chairs we had taken with us from the dining room. I read the passage for the day from *Our Daily Bread* first, and then Diana read from one of her inspirational books. We prayed and I asked God to help Diana realize how scary it must have been for her nephew, Everald, last night. As we held hands and continued to pray, Diana acknowledged in prayers how she might have been displacing some resentment she had toward her brother to his son and asked for forgiveness. We prayed alternatively about all God's blessings: the beautiful sunrise, peace, tranquility, nature, love, and for connecting with each other and reconnecting with our roots. After praying, we spontaneously got up and quietly continued to hold hands with our eyes still closed.

I heard the wind and the sound of crickets and rustling leaves. And then I no longer heard anything or felt my body. Everywhere was black, and everyone including my surroundings had disappeared. I had no presence. It was as if I fell into an abyss and didn't exist any longer. I don't know if it lasted for seconds or minutes because time and everything literally stood still for those moments. My sense of hearing was the first thing that began to return. I heard this sound, like a man's voice humming a tune, "La la, la la, la la, la, la la la, la," repeatedly. It sounded familiar, but I could not recognize it at the time. Then I started to feel Diana's hands and then my body again. Later, I remembered the tune. It was "Holy, holy, holy, Lord God Almighty." This experience was surreal and entirely blissful. What had just happened to me? Did I just have an out-of-body experience?

I started to ask Diana if she had heard the man singing. She looked at me strangely and said in her usual blunt style, "Dave, it's just me and you. Nobody not singing. Only graves down there." It suddenly dawned on me that what she was saying was true. There were three graves with white tombs: one for my grandmother, Sistah; one for Aunt Vie, my grandaunt; and one for cousin, Trevor, who was killed in America, and his body was buried here after it was shipped back home. Nothing else but the graves and the vegetation were down there. I wanted to tell Diana about my out-of-body experience, but I couldn't. I needed to process it for myself first.

I remembered Trevor, who was the only child of my mom's eldest sister, who everyone called Sister Florence. He had popped up on the scene in New York and came by to see my mom. One day, he stopped by when I was there, and we started to relate. Although he had just been in the country for a couple of months, he was holding down his own and essentially just stopped by to pay us a visit as a family. He grew up in the Tower Hill section of Kingston that is part of the hood, and he was sort of a rebel. Being around him kind of reignited my rebellious nature as well, and we were soon hanging out together. Everyone in the family knew what he was into, including my mother. His apparently quick success could only be attributed to the selling of drugs. Crack was not yet on the scene, and most Jamaicans were not into selling hard drugs like heroin and cocaine.

I was around twenty-one at the time and was driving a little beat-up Fiat that I used for going to work and to get around town. Trevor wanted me to help him find a spot to do his business. He was looking for a store to front as a record shop to sell marijuana. One day on my way to work, I found the ideal spot on Gun Hill Road right off Webster Avenue, a boarded-up storefront with a For Rent sign. It was right down the hill from North Central Bronx Hospital where I worked. He had me call the telephone number listed on the sign and arranged to meet the owner who wanted a deposit and one month rent in advance.

We met with the owner, paid him the rent and deposit, and told him we were going to be opening up a record shop. There was another record shop at the corner of the next block that was also a front for selling weed, but it didn't matter. There was enough business for everyone to go around. Trevor had a real, professional-looking sign made—Gun Hill One Stop. He said he didn't want to call it a record shop because he also wanted to stock novelties, household items, and foodstuff like peanuts, potato chips, gums, candies, and so forth. We picked up some records from a wholesale Jamaican record store on White Plains Road in the Bronx, located in walking distance from our store and got the other items from the Bronx Terminal Market.

I was doing a lot of running around with Trevor and picking up supplies, but who was going to stay in the store? I was working at the hospital and would only be available in the evenings after work and on weekends. Even though I was a Rasta with dreads and easily fit the stereotype, I wasn't the weed-selling type. I was in my early twenties. I had completed two years of college at the John Jay College of Criminal Justice and had never been arrested and wasn't planning to either. Trevor told me not to worry, that he had somebody and, later that day, introduced me to this kid named Ricky. He was very slim, around twenty-two, but looked like a little kid. I could tell from the way he spoke that he was from Kingston and also from the hood. He was already briefed by Trevor and knew exactly what to do. He also introduced me to Cassandra, an African American woman who appeared to be in her mid—to late twenties. She was from Harlem and seemed to be very nice at the time. She knew the streets and was helping Trevor get around, especially when I wasn't available. It was obvious that she and Trevor had something going.

They would always have to take a taxi whenever they had to go somewhere, and Trevor wanted to buy a car but didn't have his papers (green card). Cassandra had a brother who died during his childhood, and Trevor was able to take over his identity and use his birth certificate and social security to get his license. One day, Trevor came over to my house to get me in a black BMW. All I could say was "Wow!" I asked him where he got it, and he told me he bought it from a man and that he paid him nine thousand dollars in cash for it. I think he knew I wanted to drive it, and before I could ask, he threw me the keys and said, "Go ahead. You can drive." He sat in the passenger seat beside me, and we drove over to the store. I had never driven anything that even felt close to this before; it was all in the suspensions, and the car just seemed to hug the road. *One day, I am going to own one of these,* I promised myself.

The four of us—Trevor, Cassandra, Ricky, and myself—were basically moving in the same circle and running the business. Ricky was in the store from open to close and stayed in the rear of the store behind the counter with a thick bulletproof-glass type of partition, where he would sell nickel bags of marijuana. Very few, if any, records or other items in the store were ever sold. Trevor was always traveling with or running errands for the mysterious Mr. T (who none of us ever met) and would only come there a few days a week for a couple hours. Sometimes, I would walk down there on my lunch hour from the hospital, which was a few blocks away; but most of time, I went there after work and hang out with Ricky. At times, all four of us would be there together (especially when the store first opened); and other times, it would be just Ricky, Cassandra, and me. Most of the time, it would be only Ricky there by himself.

Trevor told me he still wanted to get his papers and knew the quickest way would be to marry an American citizen or someone with a green card. "Why don't you marry Cassandra?" I asked facetiously, anticipating a negative response.

"Dat pum-pum have too much mileage. Mi want a nice likle yard ting, mon," he said as we both broke out in laughter. She wasn't exactly ugly, but she had a loud mouth and was built like she could kick both our asses.

She reminded me of this girl that I had a fight with in high school. It was September, and I had just begun going to school in America for the first time. They started me off in the tenth grade, and although I was fourteen, I was little and looked a lot younger than my age. On my first day in art class, there was this girl who looked exactly the opposite: she was big and appeared a lot older. I remembered thinking that old people must be allowed to go to high school in America and that she must be somebody's grandmother. I don't know what happened, but she must've seen me looking at her (or probably read my mind) because out of nowhere, she started to curse and threaten me in front of the teacher and the whole class.

"I going to kick your little West Indian ass," she said. "You just wait till the bell rings." I hadn't made any friends yet, so I was alone. I was terrified and scared that I was going to be torn to pieces by a four-hundred-pound gorilla.

"Lord, help me," I prayed silently while I continued to do my artwork, trying to act brave. She continued, "Yeah, you just wait till the bell rings, you little West Indian motherfucker." I thought to myself, *The teacher is going to save me. I know it. She heard her threaten me. I'm just a baby. She's not going to allow her to kill me.*

Rrrring! The bell rung. I waited for everyone to leave the class first and for the teacher who just left me and walked over to the door. Grandma and the rest of the class were waiting outside the door for me. I waited for the teacher to tell everyone to go to class and for her to tell the girl to leave me alone. But to my astonishment, instead of helping me, Ms. Shapiro joined the crowd and was waiting like everyone else—to see me get my ass kicked.

God, there was nobody to save me. I was happy living in Jamaica, and now after living only two months in America, I'm going to die. My whole life flashed in front of me—all fourteen years of it. I thought how I never got a chance to say good-bye to my parents and how I would never get to see beautiful Jamaica again. It was time; she was coming at me. I felt my back touch the wall, and everything around me seemed to be in slow motion. I couldn't see or hear anyone, only a huge object coming toward me. *Pow!* Everything turned red, and blood was spewing all over the place.

I must have popped a blood vessel. Her face was full of blood, and the next thing I know, someone was holding me. I heard Ms. Shapiro shouting to the monitor, "Take him to the dean." I was brought downstairs to the dean's office and put into a room where the monitors stood guard. Several minutes later, I overheard someone in the next room say the school nurse was able to stop the bleeding but that she was going to be taken to the hospital because she had lost a lot of blood.

The dean came into the room and, without asking me anything (not even my name), told me to go home and not to come back to school without my parents. The next day, my parents and I went back to see the dean. We were accompanied by Ms.

Singleton, a neighbor, who acted as our spokesperson and would speak on our behalf. She was African American and was actually the person who had registered me to the school a few weeks earlier. Not knowing what to expect, my mom and dad were extremely nervous. Ms. Singleton was very jovial and relaxed with the dean, which somehow made this tense situation a bit easier for everyone. The dean said that I would be suspended for one week and that I was lucky the other student didn't want to press any charges.

Me in the Bronx a few days after arriving from Jamaica

*   *   *

Occasionally, Trevor would sometimes come over to the house when there were other family or friends who had stopped by to visit me or my mom. On this particular day, my sister, Pheobe, and her friend, Sharon, were visiting. Sharon was Jamaican and a cutie with a dark skin and a nice little body. I don't think it was necessarily a setup, but my sister introduced them to each other, and they both hit it off right away. Trevor would offer her a ride home and find out she had her papers and didn't have a man. Everyone kind of anticipated what would happen next. A few weeks later, they were married and lived together as man and wife.

Cassandra knew the deal and was associated with everyone in Trevor's circle (except for the mysterious Mr. T). She knew my family and that he had married Sharon. However, everyone knew that Trevor was still involved with her the same as before. Ricky and I had become good friends, and we knew she didn't care for either us. She acted like she was competing with us for Trevor's attention, and we suspected she was just an opportunist and was only concerned about herself. One afternoon, I was in the back of the shop with Ricky, helping him bag out some weed when a cop walked in. I started to sweat and thought for sure this was it. This was a bust, and we were going to go jail.

Earlier, before I got there, Ricky apparently had an argument with Cassandra and told me she had stormed out of the store. Ricky was just as shocked as I was when the cop walked into the store. I was not sure what he was thinking, but before the cop even said anything, Ricky shouted, "We don't have anything to hide, and you can search if you want." I thought to myself, *What the heck are you saying to the police, fool.* Instantaneously, I regained my bearings and said, "How can I help you, Officer?" The cop answered, "We got a call about somebody with a gun in here." I said, "No, Officer, there is nobody with a gun in here."

He didn't say anything else, and I was relieved when he just turned around and started walking toward the exit. As the officer headed to the door, I noticed how he was eyeballing everything in the store. And right then, I knew the inevitable would happen. The police will be back; it was just a matter of time. Until this day, I don't understand why the cop came by himself because

New York's finest always travel in pairs—especially with a call about somebody with a gun. That was pretty unbelievable.

The thought of being in the store and getting busted was always at the back of my head, but it wasn't until I was faced with the situation with the cop that I realized I was playing with my freedom and, ultimately, my future. I walked out of the store literally seconds after the cop had left, thinking how devious Cassandra was and how lucky I was that this was not a true bust. As I walked down Gun Hill Road and across Webster Avenue, I continued thinking about how close this call was and how much my life would have changed if I had gotten arrested. Right then and there, I decided that I was never going to go back to the store. I knew that it would be just a matter of time before the police would come back. I was right. A few days later, the store was raided by the police, and Trevor, Ricky, and my sister, Phoebe, were taken to jail.

Trevor seemed to be going out of town more frequently, and we would see Sharon at the house with my sister more often than usual. She was like part of the family now, and my mom loved her and treated her like a daughter. I will never forget this particular day around one o'clock in the morning when Sharon called. I had fallen asleep but was awakened by the phone. I picked up the extension in my room and heard her screaming to my mother on the phone that Trevor was kidnapped by two gunmen. She said she heard Trevor pulled into the driveway, and when she looked through the bedroom window, she saw two men who came out of nowhere with guns and they got into the car with him and told him to drive. I remained silent and could not recall what I was thinking but remembered my mother saying, "Jesus Christ."

Later that evening when I came home from work, I went into the kitchen where my mother was. The radio in the kitchen was tuned to 1010 WINS, a twenty-four-hour news station. Right after I said hello, I heard the announcer report that a body was found somewhere in Brooklyn. Standing beside her, I heard my mother repeat, "Lord Jesus," and knew she believed it was Trevor's. "Come on, Mom. How do you know that's Trevor?" She didn't answer me but walked away, weeping. The next day, Phoebe and Sharon went to the medical examiner to look at the body. My mother was right; it was Trevor.

Sweetie, Come Brush Me

It was hot the night I arrived, so I had slept in my boxers and had stayed in them during the meditation and throughout most of the morning. I went out and sat on the veranda with Diana and Papa and could see the schoolchildren in their uniforms on their way to school. The girls were wearing different variations of blue and white, depending on the school they were attending while the boys just wore khakis. I didn't see any of the little boys wearing short pants to school like I did when I was a youngster in Jamaica and just thought, *Well, that was then.* There were women skillfully balancing baskets filled with produce on their heads, older men walking in water boots with machetes in their hands, and other folks dressed up, going to work.

A small pickup filled with mangoes was passing by. Diana jumped up as the man on the back of the pickup shouted, "Mango. Mango. Fifty dollar a dozen!" I instinctively followed her to the pickup and watched her negotiate see how much "brawta" (extra mangoes) she could get for her money. "These mangoes are from St. Elizabeth," the man told her. "Oh really. Well, up here, a dozen is fourteen." They laughed, and the man gave her two extra mangoes. Suddenly, I became very self-conscious as it dawned on me I was walking around in the middle of the street with my boxer shorts underwear. I said to Diana, "Oh sweats, I'm in my drawers." She laughed and said, "Like anybody really cares." It didn't seem to matter to anyone, and I decided not to let it bother me either as I kept on joking and laughing with Diana, and the man with the mangoes on the back of the pickup.

Everald was getting ready to go to school, and Diana told him to bring his khaki uniform to her so she could iron it for him. I could see that she was sorry about the way she treated him the night before and was trying to lay on him some TLC (tender loving care). He came into the kitchen where I was and poured hot water from a thermos over a tea bag into a metal mug. He added some sugar from a jar and a little condensed milk from a can with a picture of a cow on it, stirred it with a spoon, and started to sip it. I asked if that was all he was going to have for breakfast, and he said yes. I said, "By the way, where were you last night?" He looked at me and said, "Huh?" I repeated it in patois, "A weh you did deh last night?" He answered, "Roun' a Mikey."

*   *   *

Diana and Joan live in the same apartment complex in Kingston, and Diana allowed Joan to use her car while she is away in New York. Because we arrived in Montego Bay, we had to depend on local transportation to get around. We planned on going into Mandeville to check out the Northern Caribbean University (formerly West Indies College), a Seventh-day Adventist school. Since I was in the area, I wanted to check out the high school to see if it was somewhere I would want to send my son, Michael, as I heard it had a good reputation and turned out successful alumni. We had to take a minibus from Craig Head to Christiana and then take another minibus to Mandeville. As soon as we left the house and stepped through the gate, Diana flagged down this minibus we saw making its way around the bend. As we boarded the bus, I had no clue what was in store ahead on my ride into Mandeville.

The Parish of Manchester is situated inland on one of the most mountainous region of the island, and Craig Head is located near the highest point in Manchester. The roads were very narrow and curvy. If a car was coming from the opposite direction, the other vehicle had to slow down or had to come to a complete stop in order for the other vehicle to pass. The precipitous mountainside with its spiral-shaped roads curved so deep it was hard to tell if anything was coming from the opposite direction, and some drivers would toot their horns before coming around the curve. All the vehicles seemed to travel in a zigzag fashion, going down the mountain until reaching leveler ground in Christiana.

Due to the obvious danger involved in maneuvering a vehicle on the mountainside, one would expect the drivers would be more cautious and would travel at safer speeds, but that was not the case. Because they wanted to make more money, the taxi drivers travel at unthinkable speed back and forth to Christiana. Every time they get back to Christiana, the driver would pack his vehicle so much that some of the passengers were literally sitting on one another before he would take off again. Everyone understood that the driver was trying to make a living, and nobody complained. The ride felt like a roller coaster but was twice as dangerous.

Highway Catastrophe

The last time I visited Jamaica was several years ago, and I was with my wife and our two little boys. My wife and the boys were spending a few days in Negril with my wife's sister, and I was staying at my cousin Cynthia in Christiana. On my way back to pick them up, we observed an oil tanker ablaze about one hundred yards on the highway ahead of us. The tanker was jackknifed and was blocking the highway, and we saw the driver running away and coming toward us. He told us a minibus coming from the other direction tried to overtake another vehicle around the curve and ran into his oil tanker. He said he was fleeing because he felt the tanker might explode. As a nurse, I felt I had to do something to help anyone that might have survived the accident. So my cousin Sherdon, who was driving me around, and I left our car and ran over to the scene of the accident.

What we encountered was the most devastating thing I had ever witnessed in my life: There were mangled bodies thrown from the minibus with such force that brain matter was splattered on the asphalt. There was a young boy around ten years old with a faint pulse, but his head was smashed so badly on the road that it was doubtful he would survive. There was nothing I could do; I felt completely helpless. A crowd had now started to gather, and a man drove up in a pickup truck, asking people to help put some of the accident victims on the back so he could take them to the hospital. Although I knew from my training as a nurse that moving accident victims without stabilizing them first could cause more damage, I still assisted in putting some of the victims on the back of the pick up. There would be no airlift or paramedics, and this represented the only chance of survival, if anyone was going to make it. Later, I heard on the news that there were no survivors.

I thought about this terrible accident as we left Christiana and started our next roller coaster ride into Mandeville. Diana was aware of how I was feeling and started to sing her version of our Lord's Prayer, "Owa Fada, hoo hart in haaven. Haloowed be thy name." I became more relaxed as I started to laugh and gain more confidence as we continued the trip into Mandeville.

The high school was renamed the Victor Dixon High School and was located on a different campus from the college. It was only a short distance away, but we were told to take a shuttle bus into town and then to take a taxi up to the school. Just as we were to get into a taxi, we saw Desrene walking down the road toward us. She said she was on her lunch break and would accompany us up to the school. In the taxi, she told us that she had a student boarding with her from the high school and that he was an American. She said she knew her way around the school quite well and that she would introduce us to the principal.

The school secretary escorted us to a large room across the principal's office where she asked us to have a seat. She said she would let us know as soon as the principal becomes available. At the other end of the room, there was a group of about five students talking with two adults who appeared to be either faculty or guidance counselors. Desrene said her boarder was over there, and from the expression on his face, he looked like he was in some kind of trouble. Desrene left us where we were sitting and headed over to the group. She spoke briefly with the two adults and to her boarder and then rejoined us. She started to tell us how difficult it was with her boarder when he first came to stay with her and how she was finally able to reach him. She said he started making such a good adjustment that even his parents began to marvel at his progress. She didn't discuss the reason why he was being counseled at this time along with four of his peers, and we didn't ask.

Before meeting with the principal, we were asked to meet with the assistant principal, Ms. McClean. She was nicely dressed, dark-skinned, and appeared to be in her forties. I started telling her I was here to check out the school as I had heard good things about it and that I was considering sending my son there. She surprised me when she looked straight into my eyes and asked, "Why do you want to send him here?" She explained that a lot of parents from the United States bring their children to the school because they can't control them at home and that some of the children had been to jail in the States and had a history of violence, which the parents conveniently forget to tell the school after dropping them off there. She added that the information about the student's past was usually revealed by the students themselves after they got in trouble. Ms. McClean continued to tell us that fourteen out of the sixteen students who were admitted to the school from the United States last year had to be sent home.

We eventually met with the principal, Mr. Johnson, who more or less reiterated what Ms. McClean had said. We asked him about the faculty and about the school's academics. He said he had a mostly full-time and a couple part-time teachers and that some of the faculty were actually students from the college. He said the school takes in students from the seventh grade until the twelfth grade, and as it is owned by an American organization, the students receive a diploma similar to those issued in the United States. He asked me how old my son was, and I told him he was thirteen and would be starting the eighth grade in September. He said it would have been better if he had started there in the seventh because the younger they are, the easier it is for the school to mold them. I agreed but told him I needed more time to prepare.

I actually started to have second thoughts after the meeting with Ms. McClean. I knew it was going to be difficult to sell the idea to my wife, and I wasn't sure if I wanted to put Michael in such an unpredictable environment. He gave me an application and gave us a tour of the school before we left. On our way back, we stopped off at Desrene's workplace and walked into town where I made an international call back home to my wife and the boys in New York.

About a year later after returning home to New York, Diana called and told me Desrene's boarder had been killed. He and one of the local boys in the town had a fight when the boy called him a batty man, and he was stabbed to death. After we got back from our trip from Mandeville that evening, we roasted corn on the cob outside on a bonfire while chitchatting with a man around Papa's age. He acted and looked like he was in his fifties, but he was most likely in his seventies. Before going to sleep that night, I read the introduction to Dennis Forsythe's book, *Rastafari*, where he discussed the concept of Anancyism.

The Third Day

The next morning, we took the early bus to Kingston. We left Craig Head at 4:00 AM and arrived in Kingston at 7:30 AM. On the bus, every seat (in fact, every space) had been taken, plus there were people hanging off the side of the bus. During the trip, Diana and I spoke about the concept of Anancyism and how it plays out in Jamaican society. Every Jamaican knows about Br'er Nancy from Anancy stories and is therefore quite familiar with his shenanigans. You will often hear a Jamaican say to another Jamaican on the island, "Yu a play Br'er Nancy pon me," that means, "You are trying to outsmart me."

The main reason for me going to Kingston was to see Mr. Forsythe, an attorney, to give him some papers. Diana had recommended him to me to do the legal work for the sale of our property in Maverley. We had a buyer, and he needed me to provide information on my father's estate in order to complete the sale.

Dennis Forsythe was an academic and had taught at Howard University before returning to Jamaica to teach at the University College of the West Indies. According to Diana, because his ideas were too radical for some of his students and colleagues alike, they conspired and petitioned the university to strip off his professorship thereby ruining his career. His brother, an attorney, helped in facilitating his transition into becoming an attorney.

We got to Joan's house a few minutes to eight and before she left for work. We hadn't seen each other in a long time, and we hugged and embraced each other like long lost cousins. She is a teacher, and she said although her students were off from school today, she had to go to work because her school was still open. David's school was open, but Joan told him to stay home and babysit his younger brother, Rasheed, and his cousin, Navaro. David and Rasheed stayed with Joan until every other weekend or so when their mom flew down. Then they would go to their own apartment, which was located in the same complex at Garden Estates near the National Stadium. David was attending Wolmer's Boys High School while Rasheed attended a local elementary school. Diana believed both her boys were brilliant, and she wanted them to be educated in Jamaica.

David had grown since the last time I saw him, which was around a year ago, and he was around five feet ten. They literally knocked me over when they saw me. David tried to lift me up while Rasheed jumped on my back, toppling me and causing all three of us fall to the ground. I also met Joan's family. Her daughter, Maria, was sixteen and her son, Navaro, was five. Her husband, who everyone called T, said that he had heard so much about Uncle Dave from David and Rasheed, that he was finally glad to meet me.

This is Joan, Diana's sister in her classroom

Back to School

Diana changed into shorts and tank tops, and I borrowed a pair of shorts and a T-shirt from David. We were going to drop Joan off at her school and then drive to the National Stadium where we would go jogging. On the way back from Joan's school, we drove north on Marescuax Road and passed Mico Teacher's College and Mico Practising Primary and Junior High. I saw some children going to school in their uniforms and told Diana to turn left into the road leading to the school. Mico Practising is where I went to school before going to America, and I just wanted to see it again.

As I walked through the gate looking around at the campus, which composed of the teacher's college and the practicing school, I became very self-conscious. It wasn't just about my surroundings but also what I was wearing. I guess it was a kind of a "holy ground" experience I was feeling, but Diana said I looked all right. It was not a regular school day as the school was getting ready to close for their summer holiday, and the senior class would be graduating in a few days. The school was shaped like a rectangle with an open space in the middle. In the morning before classes begin, all the students would stand outside their classrooms for morning devotion followed by any announcements. This is where the principal would also address any issue of importance pertaining to the student body as a whole.

I walked into the school and was aware they had just completed morning devotion and was returning to class. The first person I spoke to was a young woman who was a teacher. I started to tell her about my interest and my history with the school, but she said she was in a hurry and that she would take me to the office. As I was being escorted over to the office, I passed some of the classrooms where I was once taught as a student and could see the students talking and laughing just as I once did. I reflected back to my days as a student in one particular classroom that I glanced into as I was passing and realized that's how I must've behaved about twenty or so years ago.

I was introduced to a nicely dressed woman standing outside the office door who was speaking to someone inside the office. She seemed genuinely fascinated with my story as I told her about my history at Mico and how I just had to stop by. I was impressed when she said she was the school's guidance counselor as the school never had a guidance counselor in my days. Although Mico Practising was considered one of the elite schools in Kingston, the teacher's strap or bamboo cane was the only guidance counselor I ever knew. She was very pleasant and introduced me to some of the teachers as she gave me a tour of my old school.

The school had expanded with the addition of an upper level and was now teaching junior high school students. The upper level was also where the school had its new computer lab. I could tell that this was one of the school's pride and joy, and I was also very impressed. She bid me farewell after walking me to the school's exit and gave me a box of half-frozen orange juice from the canteen to take with me as the day was hot. It felt as if a chapter in my life was now complete, and I knew that those recurring dreams I used to have where I never finished high school and had to return to Mico would now stop.

Little Rasheed at school on a break in his short pants

Going to Town

It was a very hot morning, but Diana waited patiently for me inside the car. We left the school and drove over to the National Stadium about a mile away. We parked the car next to the police station and did some stretching before I proceeded to power walk while Diana jogged alongside me. When we returned to the house, Diana telephoned Mr. Forsythe and told him I was here in Kingston with her and that I wanted to drop by his office. They agreed on a meeting time of 1:00 PM at his office located on Duke Street in downtown Kingston.

We were delayed leaving the house because there was no water to take a shower. David indicated he would try to look for the groundkeeper; however, when he located him, the groundkeeper told him there was a water main break and that there would be no water. I went out to talk to him, and he said the men from the water commission were working on it and that the water should be turned back on in about thirty minutes. The traffic lights were out as we drove downtown to Mr. Forsythe's office due to a power blackout. *This was not just happening in the country alone but nationwide,* I thought to myself. Traffic was backed up, and we didn't get to Mr. Forsythe's office until 2:30 PM. His secretary told us the air conditioner was not working due to the power blackout and that Mr. Forsythe had left because it was too hot for him to work. He left a message that we could meet with him at his home.

Meeting with Br'er Nancy

On the way back to the car, Diana said she wanted to stop by an associate who owned a health food store just down the road. As we walked, she told me that he had inherited the business from his uncle who passed away. She said the man had a law degree but was a typical Br'er Nancy who swindled her out of a hundred US dollars. She had brought him up some herbs from

America over a year ago, and he still had not paid her. Yet he was still trying to get her to bring him some more. She said that he just had to know how to outsmart them at their own game by being Sister Nancy, let him think he is getting over, and then you end up with more—that's how Anancyism works, and Jamaica is full of Br'er Anancies.

The health food store was also a vegetarian restaurant and appeared to be twice as large as the other stores on that street. As we walked through the open door, I could see customers eating at tables and others ordering takeouts at the counter. I noticed a slightly obese man sitting alone at his table chomping on some food. Diana continued talking and described the man as being very toxic and doesn't know the first thing about health and nutrition. We walked over to a room to the left of the counter where Diana asked for Mr. Burton. A young woman pointed to the table where I had noticed the man sitting by himself eating. Diana looked over and said, "There he is." She apparently had not seen him when we entered the store. She introduced me as her cousin and business partner and told him I was part of her nutrition and counseling business.

Diana and I had always discussed and planned to open our own business. We were both RNs but were very strong believers in herbal and alternative medicine. I had done my research including taking a course on herbal medicine. I was a disciple of Dr. Gary Null and had read some of his books including *Get Healthy Now!* I also participated in a study group he was doing about Adventism that he had conducted in my church. Although I started about two weeks late in the group that lasted for six weeks, I was amazed to witness how his protocol of diet and herbal supplements changed people's lives. I remember this older woman in particular with crippling, rheumatoid arthritis who had to use a walker. It was painful for her to walk, and it took her a very long time just to get from the church's vestibule to the main sanctuary. He filmed everyone at the start and on at the end of the study. On the last day, I witnessed this old lady run down the stairs to the lower level of the church, where they were filming, without her walker or any other ambulating device. She danced in front of the camera, and her face was beaming instead of being twisted with pain.

I could sense the "ginalship" (another Jamaican colloquial for Anancyism) that Diana was telling me about as she and the man negotiated. He was eating stewed peas and rice with some kind of meat in it that looked like pork. He was trying to convince Diana to bring more supplies from America for him and he would make her a partner in his business. I could see straight through the bull. She told him she was going into business for herself and that she already had a business partner. She attempted to tell him about our plan to start our own business in Jamaica, but he was not interested and continued to eat while expressing his own agenda.

I could tell Diana had had enough and was ready to leave when she asked him in her own Dianesque fashion, "By the way, how can you be eating that kind of food in your business?" We weren't quite ready for the answer he gave us and laughed when he said, "You know, you have to give the stomach what it calls for sometimes." This food was a special kind of medicine only for Br'er Anancy. Burton seemed to also have a romantic interest in Diana and, before we left, tried inviting her out to dinner "to discuss some more business." She declined his invitation and told him that would be difficult as she was really here as my escort and that I had a lot of grounds to cover in only a few days, which was technically the truth.

The traffic lights were still out as we traveled uptown to see Mr. Forsythe who lived in an exclusive part of St. Andrew. I knew we were heading north toward Red Hills but was a little disoriented as I couldn't recognize what route we were taking. I was glad Diana was my self-designated escort and chauffer that made getting around the island a lot easier for me. We made a left turn off the main road and drove into what appeared to be some kind of an estate. This was definitely a ritzy neighborhood and could probably be one of the richest parts of the island where all the people with money lived. There were no more signs of poverty that was noticeable only a few moments before we turned off the main road. There were homes with swimming pools, Jags, and Mercedes in their driveways. The homes were ranch style and beautiful with palm and mango trees everywhere. Red Hills is located at the crest of the mountains of St. Mary, bordering the northern section St. Andrew and felt a little cooler than in Kingston.

Mr. Forsythe lived in one of the more modest home in the area, and when we arrived, there was a brown Corolla parked in his driveway. The gate was open, and we drove right in and parked behind the Corolla. We stepped onto the veranda from the driveway and knocked on the door. Mr. Forsythe, who was dressed comfortably in shorts and a T-shirt, answered the door. He appeared to be in his forties, of average height and built, and had a dark-brown complexion. Initially, I felt a little intimidated by his presence but became more relaxed as we began to talk. He had a pleasant manner and smiled easily. I told him I started to read his book. "Which one?" he asked, looking kind of puzzled. I was unaware he had authored more than one book, and Diana blurted out, "*Rastafari,*" before I could say it. We got into some deep conversation about Anancyism, and he pointed out how it even influenced the legal system in Jamaica.

Up to this point, I had only read the introduction to *Rastafari* and the first chapter where he wrote that he considered himself to be a Rasta man. I told him about my involvement with the Rastafarian religion and that at one time, I even wore dreadlocks. "Once a Rasta, always a Rasta," he said kind of jokingly. He then pulled out a brown paper bag from the library next to where he was sitting and said, "I'm a Rasta man and love to smoke my weed, you know. Would you like some?"

"Oh no, I get too relaxed after I smoke and wouldn't be able to get anything done for the rest of the day," I said. The truth was it had been several years since I smoked marijuana, and I wasn't sure how it would make me act. Diana declined also. Her excuse was that she had a drug test coming up on her job and didn't want to chance it. "But please go ahead," I said. We watched as he cut up a little of his stash and rolled it into a small spliff. He took a few puffs after lighting up and again offered it to me. No. I shook my head. He said that he believed ganja was not only good for the soul but good for you physically as well.

At the time, I didn't understand what he was talking about until I completed reading his book *Rastafari*. In it he mentioned his personal experience with marijuana and how it helped cure him of his debilitating illnesses (physical as well as psychological). In it he said, by "sipping the cup," he was able to loosen up his ribcage, which caused his lungs and breath to be deepened thereby locating a number of blockages in his system. He continued to write, "Herbal meditations allowed me to follow the smoke into my lungs, and into my heart, legs, toes or any other part of my body, and allowed me to know these parts by feeling them out and generating vibrations in these parts. By means of such internal concentration, focus, and movements which the smoke sustained and generated, I was able to see, feel, and actually identify and touch the internal blockages within my personal system."

"Sipping the Cup"

In my early twenties, it was a natural inclination for me to become a Rastafarian as most of my friends were dreads and accepted His Imperial Majesty Haile Selassie I as Jah, the true and living God. "Sipping the cup" to me was sort of an unofficial initiation of being a true dread. From the time I lived in Jamaica, I knew that smoking weed was an important part of the Rastafarian culture and realized that one day, I would have to be truly initiated by smoking the chillum pipe if I was to call myself a true dread. The pipe itself is made from a coconut bowl with a funnel and a rubber or plastic tube attached to it. The coconut bowl is filled with water that acts like a filter for the smoke and bubbles when you "sip" on the tube. The term "sipping" is really a Rasta jargon—a more accurate description would be a long hard whiff that seemed to load the lungs to its maximum capacity.

A number of dreads would gather together (usually five to seven), remove their head coverings while giving praises to HIM, and chant psalms. Then the herb is meticulously prepared by the hosting dread who moistens it with a little water and cuts it up. A little tobacco is usually added for flavor. When this smoke is exhaled, nothing is visible but a white cloud of smoke that fills the air. Although I know this cannot be the case but every time I witness this ritual, I seem to see smoke coming, not only from the smoker's mouth and nostrils, but also from his ears and eyes as well until his whole face disappears in the cloud of smoke. I honestly never believed I would be able to tolerate that much smoke and just knew I would die a very painful death from choking. Yet I knew the day was coming when I had to partake.

The day arrived sooner than I had anticipated after me and two other dreads went to visit an elder dread named Ras Ben. This particular visit was fairly routine as it was not unusual for us to go check other dreads we know in the area just to light up a spliff or two and to socialize. We saw another dread we know from the neighborhood hanging out at Ras Ben's. He was an older dread like Ras Ben and had the locks to prove it. His locks did not reach his butt like Ras Ben's but resembled a tree with branches shooting out in all directions. As with Ras Ben, you could tell his locks took years, if not decades, to form.

After socializing for a while, Ras Ben opened a rolled-up sheet of newspaper containing some herbs. Immediately, I knew what was up and dreaded (no pun intended) what was about to take place. Although I wasn't prepared for what was about to transpire, I might as well be up to the challenge as there was no way out at this point. With lights dimmed and curtains drawn, it would soon be time. While the dreads prepared the herb and chanted psalms that always seemed to end with everyone shouting, "Jah, Rastafari!" or "Selassi I, King of Kings, Lord of Lords, Conquering Lion of the Tribe of Juda!" which were actual titles held by HIM Haile Selassi I, I positioned myself to the right of Ras Ben as the cutchie was being passed to the left-hand side. I would be the last to smoke the pipe, and by the time it got to me, it would be so watered down I could probably tolerate it. I was betting on this; it meant my survival as a dread and probably in this life.

We ended our visit with Mr. Forsythe after I cleared up some business matter regarding the sale of the piece of property in Maverley. We turned on to the main road after leaving Mr. Forsythe's place and were soon back into the true everyday Jamaican reality again. We went back to the apartment where Diana cooked up some vegetarian dishes.

Embracing Rastafari

The sun was still shining bright in the early evening hours, and I wanted to visit Maverley where I used to live as a kid growing up on the island. I wanted to see Henry and his mother, Whitey, and meet the people living in our old house. I told Diana this, but she stated quite plainly she was not going to take me to Maverley. We were standing on the balcony next to her apartment on the second floor and saw T pulling into his driving space across the road. I followed her as she walked downstairs and asked him if he would take me to Maverley.

T was driving a large company-owned late model Ford pickup with a double cabin. He was an ex-soldier and was now working as chief of security for a private company. He was average built, about six feet two, and in his midthirties. He wore a dark custom-tailored pants and a white Oxford shirt with a tie and folded a portion of his shirt over his right hip to conceal the 0.9 mm Glock he was carrying. T agreed to take me to Maverley, and while he was driving me there, we talked about his job in security, my job as a parole officer in New York, politics, and the current state of affairs in Jamaica. As we traveled and talked, I kept looking around for familiar landmarks but to no avail and couldn't help but feel like a stranger in my own country. I had been living in New York for over twenty years, and my visits to the island were few and far between.

I began feeling a little anxious when we passed St. Mary's Anglican Church and knew that we were approaching Maverley. I soon began recognizing some other places: the two gas stations on opposite sides of Washington Boulevard and the bakery on Molynes Road were still there. *Yes! I'm here,* I thought, and I told T to turn left on Westmain Drive. As we entered the little village, we passed the park on the left and the ball field across the road on the right then Ogden Crescent, where the post office used to be; after that, the three shops on the left followed by Kempton Avenue; and next was Clarion Road where I used to live. The road was hairpin-shaped without any outlet, and T made a U-turn around the circle before coming to a stop at the gate of the old house I was pointing to. It was now getting into twilight time with the sun feeling a little less intense as the sky began to change into a bright magenta-orange color.

Although I had been living abroad for many years and had visited Maverley in the past, this time was different; it felt more like a sort of homecoming. There were children playing on the street and people standing at their gates. I immediately recognized Dolly Black and Ms. Claire who everyone called Baby Mother because (you got it) she has a lot of kids. "Baby Mother," I called out. "Who is that calling me?" she inquired. When I answered, "It's Dave," she recognized me right away and started to ask me about my mother, my sister, my brother, my niece, and my nephew all by their names. I considered it remarkable that she remembered everybody and me after all these years. After a few minutes of asking each other about how everybody was doing, I walked over to Dolly standing within hearing distance at her gate right next door. "How are you, Ms. Dolly?" I greeted her. "Fine, thank you. How's Ms. Heron?" "She's OK," I replied. They wanted to know if my mother was visiting too, and I told them I was just here by myself.

Something remarkable began to happen while I was speaking to Ms. Dolly: All the little children who were playing on the street came over to where I was standing and started to flock me. I turned around and noticed they had formed a circle around me and two of them started holding my hands. This took me quite by surprise, and I really didn't know what to think. They were not begging me for anything, and I'm quite sure this wasn't the first time these children had seen someone visiting from abroad, so what was going on? I decided to stop thinking and just stay in the moment. They were smiling and staring into my face and I in theirs (this was another moment of bliss), and it was all love. This little girl continued holding my hand and wouldn't let go, and I felt so wonderfully connected to her, the surroundings, and all the other children following me around.

Twilight had now totally settled in, and I could see the gigantic sun starting to go down over the horizon, its beautiful orange glow overwhelming everywhere and everything: the ground, the cars, the homes, the trees, and even the eyes. The kids followed me over to Henry's house, but he was not home. I spoke to Mrs. White, his mother, who everybody called Whitey, and she went through the same ritual: "How's everybody—Ms. Heron, Barrie, Phoebe, Willy, and Jacky" and "Are you here by yourself" greetings again. The children were still there with me with the little girl holding my hand and still looking up to my face.

As much as I try, I cannot find words to truly express how I was feeling; it was all so surreal. Although I didn't understand what was really happening, somehow I felt there were (some) spiritual forces working with me ever since I got on the island. It was at this point that I thought about keeping a diary to record all my experiences and further adventures that would continue to unfold during this trip to Jamaica.

T was leaning on the back of the pickup with his arms folded and seemed a little annoyed at the children following me around. I could sense he was on a different type of wavelength as he barked at one of my little angels to leave me alone. Although I had been there for less than an hour, it felt as if time had stopped for me. But my mind was telling me it was now time to leave. Maybe it was because of T's uneasiness. Before leaving, I wanted to meet the McClouds who occupied the property where I used to live, but only the wife was home. She was standing at the gate, and I introduced myself to her and told her I had met with the lawyer and had given him the papers to finalize the sale of the property. She was polite and was apparently relieved to hear that she and her husband was about to finally own that piece of property they had called home for the past several years. Before leaving, I gave

Diana's telephone number to Mrs. White for Henry to call me, and then I said good-bye to everyone. It was now sunset.

Henry at age 4 and Me at age 9

The Fourth Day

The next day, before we went jogging, Diana had gotten in touch with one of her old classmates from the University College of the West Indies at Mona Heights and wanted to visit her. Diana said the beach was right there and that I could dress in my swim trunks that I could also use for my jogging outfit. She lived in Mountain View, which was an exquisite neighborhood in Kingston, and her home was just a stone's throw away from the airport. The house was nice and big with the den's opening to the driveway. In the back, at the right of the house, was a large swimming pool and a wall that separated the house from the beach. There was a little gate in the wall giving access to the beach.

Avnell greeted us at the door and was cordial and polite. She was a very petite woman with long African braids that looked like extensions but were salt-and-pepper and probably authentic. The furniture in the den was straw and white finished with fluffy floral cushions on all the seats. As we sat down, I could hear the gushing waves of the ocean on the beach. Diana had not told me much about her, but from what I observed, I imagined she must be very well-to-do. She still appeared a little sleepy with puffy eyes that she occasionally wiped with the back of her hands. Diana had told me to bring my Bible, and I also took my *Daily Word* and *Our Daily Bread* magazines with me. Diana had taken one of her books on meditations with her.

We started to talk, and I found out she had a degree in nutrition and that she had a spiritual side to her. We discussed different topics including Anancyism and the violence that existed in Jamaica today. Diana said how it appeared I had discovered the feminine side of me—which was loving, caring, and spiritual—and that her dad was home alone and able to wash, cook, and take care of himself while her mother was away spending time with her sister, Dimple, in Washington. Avnell expressed how she felt Jamaican men have become marginalized in today's society. She added that Jamaican men, at one time, felt free to express their feminine side by cooking, washing, nurturing their offspring, and doing basically everything a woman could do without having any qualms about it. "Right now, my son is cleaning the house for me, but nowadays, we are not teaching our sons to do these things because we think it's women's work, and thus, men have become marginalized."

The end of our discussion just naturally evolved into spirituality, and each of us contributed something before reading from whatever written material we had with us. Avnell started first by saying in life we can only get what we want if we are willing to negotiate for it and that the person who has more than another person is just more skillful at negotiating. I was feeling those words more than hearing them coming through her mouth and felt that they were really deep. We finished off by holding hands and forming a circle while each of us said a prayer of meditation. I went first and was overcome (more like possessed) with a spirit of peace, much like I had during my "mountaintop" experience on the second day on the island. I wanted to savor this feeling as much as possible and didn't want to interrupt it by using too many words. I said, "God, I feel your presence here with us. Thank you for revealing yourself to us in so many ways."

Diana and I went through the little gate in the wall and walked over to the beach. Its white sand was sparsely covered with seashells and little coconuts from the palm trees that lined the shore. The waves were several stories high and would fiercely push us back on shore every time we went into the sea. After several attempts, we just decided to sit on the beach and allow the waves to push the sand on our feet. I'd never seen waves this huge before and started to imagine myself surfing on top of the highest waves. Trying to stay in that moment, I could only think, *Jamaica is so beautiful, and it's good to be here.*

We didn't feel the ocean was ready to welcome us, and we left several minutes later after only sunbathing. We were completely dry when we went back up the house and said good-bye to Avnell. We decided to go jogging along the beach, and Diana left her car parked on Avnell's sidewalk. The ocean was on both sides of the road, and I was power walking so fast that Diana, who was jogging, had difficulty keeping up with me and stayed several yards behind. It was as though I had wings on my feet and was literally in the midst of the Caribbean Sea. Its deep turquoise water just seemed to swallow us up on that strip of Palisados Road leading to the airport.

The Fifth Day

While in Kingston, I wanted to visit Tilly who was my half sister from my father's side. She was a couple of years younger than me and was conceived from an extramarital affair that almost destroyed my parent's marriage after it was discovered. My parents were always so in love, and it broke my mother's heart that the only man that she had ever loved could've betrayed her like that. I can remember as a child growing up (and even as an adult), my mom always used to say boastingly that after God made my father, he threw away the mold because there was not another man like him anywhere.

My dad was handsome and a gentleman, and except after leaving for America, I cannot remember him never coming home after work. After she apparently got over it and forgave him, my mom told me, "You know, Dave, for all the years we've been married, your dad had never missed one night lying next to me on his pillow." Ouch! I knew that really hurt her. I knew she blamed Tilly's mom and "those kind of women" who try to steal other women's husbands. But Tilly was my sister and didn't have anything to do with it, and I loved her.

Her telephone number must've changed because the number I was dialing was not connecting me to my sister. I called directory assistance, who like in the United States, was of no assistance. The operator was very impatient and made it seem like I was bothering her. "I don't have a number for that name in Washington Garden, sir," then dial tone. I wondered if Tilly had moved or was traveling outside the country with her family as they often do in the summertime. I had stayed with them on my last two trips to Jamaica and told Diana I think I could find the house. I said I believed the address was Nineteen Canewood Crescent and that I was going to Washington Garden to look for her. I got dressed in my Tommy Hilfiger's shorts, my oversized print T-shirt that I wore outside my jeans, my baseball cap, and my sneakers. I thought I might've looked a little too thuggish, but Diana said I looked hip and was all right.

I decided I would go to Maverley and get Henry whom I always try to visit every time I was on the island. I used to live next door to him when I was living in Maverley, and he was like my little brother. Washington Gardens was a half mile or so down the road from Maverley, and I was counting on him to go with me to help me find my sister's house as I wasn't sure where she lived. Diana dropped me off at Cross Roads where I would catch a cab. The taxi driver was a man in his early thirties. He was smoking a spliff, and his eyes were red and bloodshot.

Although I didn't feel particularly threatened because of Diana's obvious overprotective behavior toward me in front of the taxi driver, the thought did cross my mind whether this man would take me to my destination or try to rip me off. She was asking the driver how much it was going to cost to take me to Maverley and if I wanted her to pay the fare for me. I shook my head no, feeling a little embarrassed, and she turned around to go to her car as if she got the message but not before saying, "Be careful, all right?" This was actually the first time I was venturing out alone, and although I was feeling a little annoyed with her, I really understood that her behavior was just out of concern for me.

The taxi driver kept the spliff in his mouth throughout the trip to Maverley and the cab was full of smoke. I was hoping that I wouldn't get a contact high from all the smoke he was blowing to me at the back of the cab. As we traveled uptown to Maverley, he put on a reggae CD and turned it up full blast. I could barely think because of the loud music but tried to see if I could recognize any familiar landscape as he had taken a different route from that which T had used on the other trip. I could tell we were approaching Maverley when I noticed the Esso and Texaco gas stations at the intersection of Molynes Road and Washington Boulevard. I told the driver to make a left on West Main Drive and then take another left a little further down on Clarion Road. I noticed like before and thought to myself how all the houses seemed to look a lot smaller than when I was a child.

I remember when I used to attend Mico Practising, two of my classmates and I liked to hang out together after school. Sometimes we would go to the YMCA, the National Stadium, and the library on Tom Redcam Road, or we would walk to downtown Kingston. We didn't really commit any mischief, except sometimes, we would stone somebody's mango tree and would get chased by dogs or by the owner of the property when we tried to retrieve the mangoes we'd knocked off their tree.

A few times, we got close to being bitten by vicious Alsatians (German shepherds); and one time, one of us got caught by a man (an older youth, really) who was a passerby but wanted to take our mangoes. He started prying the mango away from King's hands (his first name was Richard, but we mostly called each other by surname), but he held on and wouldn't let go and decided to get a few bites off his mango while still struggling with the man.

King was still chewing after he was forced to let it go, and I'm not sure if the man knew or cared that the mango he took from him had bite marks all over it and walked away chomping the mango. There was a woman standing on her veranda across the street, observing the incident, holding her belly, and wailing with laughter. At that time, I couldn't imagine what she thought was so funny. To us, it was no fun getting robbed of that beautiful East Indian mango, which was just perfectly ripe enough for eating.

After the man had wrestled King's mango away, we kept on walking down the road and heard some type of commotion at the corner where we noticed some people had gathered. We ran over there to see what was happening and saw a man being beaten by the crowd. He was allegedly a pickpocket, or had robbed somebody and was being meted out with swift, Jamaican style justice. The man was curled up on the ground moaning and crying, while the someone was yelling, "tief, tief, lick im, lick out im rass," biff! bam! pow! as the man was being pounded. "Ouch! Ouch! ahh! Oh my god, I didn't do it, a lie dem a tell 'pon me." Slap! kick! punch! "Laad help me. A no true," the man said begging for mercy. But no one felt sorry for the poor soul who was so unfortunate to get caught in his crimes that was being dealt with on the spot by the crowd. King was the first one of us to land a kick on the man's leg, followed by Smiley then, what the heck, I got a couple of kicks in myself remembering how we had just been robbed ourselves. Serves him right.

We always ended up at somebody's home before going to our own home. King had an aunt who lived in Jones Town that was in the heart of Kingston and was next to Trenchtown where Bob Marley grew up. She was very nice and always fed us when we went there. King and my other classmate, Smiley, also lived uptown in St. Andrew in Duhany Park and Pembroke Hall respectively. Although I would sometimes follow my friends home and chill at their place for a while, I never took them to my place in Maverley, which was considered the ghetto. I didn't want them to see that I lived in a little one-room house with a cistern outside; it would be too embarrassing.

Ninety percent of the kids that went to Mico came from upper—or middle-class homes, and I just happened to fall in the other 10 percent that was considered poor. I used the term "considered" because I didn't speak or act like I was from the ghetto. It wasn't because I was wearing Mico epaulets on my uniform or that my mother never allowed me to hang out in the streets, and I was sheltered (because I was allowed to play and socialize with other children in my neighborhood), but Mico did expose me to being with children of middle—and upper-class families that I probably would not have experienced had I remained at Maverley school.

Whenever my friends said they wanted to go to Heron's house, I always found a way to dissuade them, and we would end up going to the library, the YMCA, or somewhere else. By the time we got done, it was too late to hang anymore, and it would be time for us to go home. One day though, we all ended up at my place, and I remembered King saying, "I never knew Heron was so poor." After this first experience, however, my friends came back all the time, and it didn't bother me. Somehow, I knew even then that being poor was only a temporary situation for me and that one day I would be wealthy. Yes, as a child, I did have a tremendous imagination as I believed most children do. You can call it childish dreams, intuition, or whatever, but I felt that I was on a journey. It was just a knowing that a lifetime of poverty was not my destiny and that the events of my life up to that point in time, part of which was growing up in Maverley, was just a part of a journey.

Henry was not home when I got to his house. Ms. White, his mother, said he had left earlier to take care of some business and that she wasn't sure what time he would be returning. I was a little disappointed that I didn't find Henry and felt lonely by myself. The great hoopla I had experienced on my first visit to Maverley was not there; none of the children, Baby Mother, Ms. Dolly, or anybody I knew was around.

I decided I would just walk over to Washington Gardens and try to find my sister by myself. I walked on to West Main Drive, made a left turn, and headed west to find my sister's house in Washington Gardens. As I walked through Maverley, I could see that a house was now built where the old police station was. Maverley School was still there and looked just about the same. Only the name was changed from Maverley Primary School to Maverley All-age School. I remembered going there and being sent to Mr. Withworth, the headmaster, for lashes whenever I was late for school. Sometimes, there was a line of about five or six of us waiting our turn to hold out our hands to get lashes for being just a few minutes tardy. I recalled it was always a little less embarrassing when there were other students standing in line with me and waiting their turn, and I couldn't imagine this form of corporal punishment was still being practiced today.

I continued walking through the little village where I used to live, being very present and conscious of my surroundings. I didn't feel afraid and knew there was little chance to run into somebody I knew after all these years. West Main Drive ended at Washington Boulevard, and I continued walking several yards until I crossed the little bridge over the gully where I thought Washington Gardens was, on the other side of the boulevard and south of Maverley. As I walked down the boulevard toward Washington Gardens, I could see the site where the Church of the Open Bible had been was now turned into a school. It used to be a big tent where this American preacher, his family, and his cohorts used to hold regular tent meetings. The services were very entertaining, and I remembered I used to have a lot of fun going there as a little kid in the sixties.

There were street vendors, whom the island people called "higglers," on the sidewalk selling everything from mangoes, sugarcanes, bulla to batteries, clothes, soaps and even toilet papers. I decided to ask one of them for directions just to make sure I wouldn't get lost. The woman told me I was heading in the right direction and that it was right across from the shopping center down the road. I said thank you, and she smiled and said,

"Right on," with an American twang as if to say, "I could tell that you are from America."

I was very happy when I got to the shopping center and to finally reach Washington Gardens. I couldn't wait to see my sister and my three nieces—Sherene, Kimone, and Samantha. Tilly's husband was of Indian descent, and the three girls had distinct Afro Indian features. I knew they were going to be surprised to see me, and I couldn't wait to see them. The neighborhood looked very middle-class with nice houses. I walked a couple of blocks and turned right on the street where they lived.

I wasn't sure of the house number and was doing this entirely from memory as I was convinced I would remember the house. It turned out that I was wrong because the first house I went to was not my sister's place. Some of the neighbors were tending their gardens or sitting on their verandas, so I decided to ask if they knew where my sister lived. The first person I asked was a man who gave me a very disdainful look before he said no and went into his house and locked his door. I thought he was just having a bad day and didn't take it personally as I was polite and respectful and greeted him first by saying good afternoon as people would customarily do on the island.

It didn't dawn on me what was happening until I went to a couple more people and was treated in the same fashion as the first gentleman. Nobody wanted to talk to me, much less went out of their way to help me. After getting the same treatment from basically everyone, it was obvious they were actually afraid of me. I had to ask myself, *Am I in Jamaica?* Suddenly, I became very self-conscious of my "rude boy" appearance and decided I had enough. It was time to wrap it up and leave before somebody calls the police to report there was a strange man in the neighborhood. Furthermore, it looked like it was going to rain, and there was nowhere for me to shelter.

When I was around eighteen and was living in the hood in the West Bronx, I used to check this girl who lived uptown on Barnes Avenue and 221st Street. It was during the summer, and I was driving a taxi that I had rented from my best friend's uncle in order to make some money. This particular evening, I picked up my best friend and two other friends we used to hang out with and decided to visit my girl and her sisters. We pulled up to the gate and were still sitting in the car talking when I noticed a police car pull up behind us. I was not necessarily afraid of the police, and when the officers came over and asked us what we were doing there, I told him I came to visit my girlfriend.

The car had livery plates on it, and we looked like young thugs who didn't belong in the neighborhood, and they assumed we were up to no good. One of the officers asked me for my license and registration, which I gave to him. He went back to the patrol car and returned and handed me back my documents, then told us we fit the description of some robbery suspects and that they wanted to search the car. They told us to keep our hands where they could see them, and one of the officers looked in the glove compartment and under the car seats with a flashlight.

The officer pulled out an old black pocketbook from under the front passenger seat. It was empty, had a torn zipper, was worn and dirty, and had obviously been there for a while. Even when the officers told us they were going to have to take us to the station house to check it out, I wasn't feeling nervous. My friends and I were still laughing and talking as we went with the officers in their patrol car. Even though we were in the same age group, my friends always looked up to me. It wasn't necessarily because I was in college or was more outspoken, but I believed it was because I was more of the leader of the pack, and everyone took their cue from me. If I wasn't nervous, they weren't going to be nervous.

The old station house was the Fifty-Seventh Precinct and was located on White Plains Road, only a couple of blocks away from my girl's house. They took us to the second floor and put us in this large cell. There were nobody else upstairs but us and the two young officers who brought us there. They walked away for a little while and then returned, opened the cell, and told us to empty our pockets on a table in front of the cell. Now I started to get a little nervous. In fact, it was almost panic time when I remembered I had a nickel bag of weed on me. I started sweating a little and felt the perspiration on my forehead. What am I going to do now? My friends didn't know I had it and, except for Lolli, didn't even smoke.

We all emptied our pockets except for me who didn't know what to do with the bag of weed and left it in my pocket. The officers patted us down after we emptied our pockets, and the one who patted me felt the object in my pocket, said, "Come on, take out everything," and started going through the few items everyone had put on the table. While the officers' attention was focused on the stuff on the table, I put the bag of weed in my mouth and tried to swallow it. Nickel bags were huge in those days and wasn't that easy to swallow. So I started chomping the bag in an attempt to chew and swallow it. "Did you take it out?" the officer asked me while turning toward me to see if I had. "Chump, chump, hmm mm." He noticed I was chewing on something and grabbed me from behind while his partner started punching me in the stomach. "You black motherfucker, spit it out. Spit it out." I tried to swallow, but there was no use. After a good solid punch to the diaphragm, the bag came flying out of my mouth.

They pushed us back inside the cell while still cussing and calling us everything except a child of God. "Y'all would've walked until you pulled that stupid shit," the officer who had searched me said. I felt more ashamed than hurt from the beating and was considering what I had gotten myself into now. I thought about how I had the opportunity to ditch the weed before I got to the precinct but never anticipated we would be searched. None of us were bad kids, and I didn't want my friends to get into trouble because of me. I had just completed my first year at John Jay College of Criminal Justice and, prior to that, worked for the New York City Police Department as a community service officer as part of the Model Cities Program where the Nixon administration was trying to recruit inner-city kids to become cops or firemen by having them work with those departments.

It was time for me to go into damage-control mode, and I thought that maybe I could probably use my college and past work experience with the police department to my advantage to get out of the mess I was in. I started to study the cop who said we could've walked and tried to figure him out.

"I can't go to jail, man. It would kill my mother. Listen, I'm a student at John Jay, and I used to work for Model Cities . . ."

"No, man. Once I put my hands on you, I got to lock you up."

"Let me just finish swallowing the bag, and you didn't touch me."

He walked away and, about two minutes later, took me out of the cell and led me to a small bathroom in the back. He gave me back the bag of weed I had tried to swallow before and said, "Here, swallow it." I put it back into my mouth, but I was afraid I would choke. The bag was just too large to swallow. "I can't swallow it. Let me flush it."

"All right, go ahead," he said, and I threw it into the toilet. *Gush* and all evidence was gone. He didn't say anything when I thanked him, but I interpreted the expression on his face to mean "That's all right."

We left the police station and walked the couple of blocks back to the car and left without my girlfriend knowing what had transpired or even knowing that I was there. I don't think it even fazed my friends how serious the situation we were in; any kind of arrest record would've been devastating to our future. I guessed they figured I got them into it and I would get them out of it. They were still laughing and joking as we made our way back to the West Bronx. "Chump, chump," Lolli, the clown, teased while the other two laughed.

With future Wife at friend's wedding reception

I could see Spanish Town Road, which was a few blocks south on other side of Washington Gardens, and I knew if I get there, I could take the bus or catch a cab back to Diana's place. I made haste to get there before it started raining and had to jump over a metal barricade, go through a hole in the fence to exit the neighborhood, and get to Spanish Town Road. It started to rain as soon as I got on the bus heading to Kingston.

On the bus, I asked for directions and actually felt normal again when someone answered me. Nobody seemed to be afraid of me, and I felt I was back with the average folks where I belonged.

I was told to get off at Six Miles and to transfer to another bus going to Half Way Tree. It was drizzling when I got off at Six Miles. The intersection was busy with a lot of traffic and street vendors.

The Sixth Day

It was Friday morning, and I was anxious to get back to the country. I had taken care of all my business in Kingston and had planned in advance that I would be leaving today. Kingston (actually St. Andrew) was my home, and I loved and enjoyed my stay there, but it wasn't my intention to spend that much time in Kingston. I missed the peace and tranquility of Craig Head and the countryside.

Henry called around seven o'clock in the morning and wanted to stop by before I left for the country. He said he was leaving right away and arrived about an hour later while we were packing the car. After speaking for several minutes, I gave him a twenty-dollar bill from the United States and told him I would be in touch before I leave on the Fourth of July.

When we reached Manchester, we decided to take a break in Christiana before climbing up the hill into Craig Head. We ran into Papa who was buying supplies at the market for his shop. He had just finished shopping, so we put his bags in the trunk and continued up the narrow mountain road into Craig Head. On the way, we stopped in Pike at Sister Sils, my mother's older sister, to drop off a letter with some cash from her daughter, Cousin Cynthia, who was staying in the Bronx with my mom while visiting from Jamaica.

Sister Sil's house was on a steep hill about fifty yards from the road, and one had to literally climb up a path of dirt and stones to get to her house. She was about eighty-eight or eighty-nine and kind of spunky like my mother and their eldest sister, Florence, who was around ninety. Diana, Papa, and the boys stayed in the car as I maneuvered the hilly path to the small wooden house up the hill.

"Sister Sil. Sister Sil," I called out as I approached the house. The door was open, and her head was wrapped with the kentelike cloth that most of the older women from the country still use to cover their heads, and she was dressed like she was either going or coming from somewhere. "Who dat? Dave?" I had not seen my aunt in umpteen years and had actually only seen her about three or four times in my entire life and was surprised when she answered "Who dat? Dave?" She said she had just got back from Christiana where she went to sell some pumpkin at the market. I sat down and talked with her for a little while before giving her the envelope from Cynthia.

Old country home in the meadow

Walking back down to the car, I marveled at how mentally intact she was and physically strong to be able to climb up and down that hill to her house at her age. I thanked God for her and the love I felt emanating from her, and I felt proud to be part of a legacy that had its roots from right in this area.

This area appeared to have remained basically unchanged throughout the years. Except for most of the homes now being equipped with running water from water tanks and people doing away with their old kerosene lamps for the convenience of electricity, things had not changed that much from my outsider's perspective. A lot of the young people had cell phones, but to use a landline or regular telephone, you had to go to Christiana as the area was still not wired for telephone service. This was really of no inconvenience to anyone and made it more rural and unspoiled for my benefit, selfish as it may be.

I thanked God for making it possible for me to take this trip to Jamaica and for going to Craig Head. God knows I truly needed this experience and to be away from the hustle and bustle of New York City. What serendipity. I made the trip to get a break and to investigate a boarding school for my twelve-year-old son, but instead, I was *spiritually reconnecting with my roots*—a benefit I had never anticipated.

Diana and David in front of her own house in Chistiana Manchester

David was complaining of having a sore throat while we were in Kingston but seemed all right after we had him gargle some warm salt water and had given two grams of vitamin C to take. About four o'clock the next morning, he woke me up wheezing and very short of breath. His forehead felt warm. I went and called Diana who was sleeping in an adjacent room. I asked her if David was asthmatic because he was wheezing and had difficulty breathing.

Diana jumped up and indicated he was not asthmatic and ran into the room where David was lying down. She felt his throat with her thumb and index finger and said his tonsils were a little swollen. She said she would have to go back to Kingston to take him to the doctor. "Why Kingston?" I asked. "I don't trust these doctors down here," she replied.

We had to change our plan due to David's illness, which was to return to Kingston on Monday, leave the car with Joan, and turn around and return by bus early Tuesday morning. It was also planned that on Sunday, our cousin, Vaughn (who had picked us up at the airport), would come and pick us up so we could hang out with him on his day off. I had become accustomed to being with Diana and her boys and was sorry to see them go. However, I relished the time I would be by myself and decided I would use the time to start my journal of my experience in Jamaica.

They departed around eight o'clock in the morning, and Diana had left her boom box and her Marianne Williamson inspirational tapes for me to listen to. I had taken my Walkman with some of my favorite smooth jazz and Take 6 cassettes with me from America and, during my solitude, had expected to get some rest and relaxation while enjoying the peace and tranquility of the Jamaican countryside.

I remembered passing a Seventh-day Adventist church on the night of the blackout and, as today was Saturday, considered going to church. I assumed that the divine service would begin at eleven o'clock as it does in North America but wanted to catch some of sabbath school, which started at nine thirty. I got up and started to prepare myself for church and decided I would take my little cousin, Everald, along with me. I felt a little attached to him ever since the incident with Diana when I had to run to his rescue, and I thought about the possibility of meeting someone at the church who would be willing to look out for him. I imagined a Good Samaritan taking him under his or her wing and getting to know him and his family and how this could change the direction of his life. I woke him up and made him breakfast, then I ironed our clothes while he was taking his shower. After I showered, we got dressed and walked to church.

The wooden church was painted off-white with a large satellite dish on the roof, and the church sign had the same Seventh-day Adventist insignia as in America. We arrived at around ten o'clock. Sabbath school was still in session. It was a typical Adventist-style atmosphere on the inside with the same types of quarterly lesson booklets issued in North America. Although everyone appeared polite and cordial, it was disappointing how our presence was barely recognized. We sat in the main sanctuary for a while and then took I took Everald outside after realizing that was where the children's sabbath school was being conducted.

At the end of sabbath school, they went right into divine worship after a short break, which allowed the children a time to come in and get settled. Everald came back over to where he was, sitting next to me, but something was wrong. He looked a little gray and uneasy and laid his head back on the pew. I asked him if he was feeling all right, and he began to rub his belly. The service had already started, but I felt I had to take him home as he was obviously in a lot of discomfort. I walked with him, and about fifty yards down the road, I asked him if he could get home by himself. He nodded and I turned around and went back to the church to catch the remainder of the service. A female elder had preached the sermon, and at the end of the service, she shook my hand at the door. She asked me where I was visiting from, and I told her I was Ms. Leslie's nephew and that I lived in New York.

I had never gone to church while I was on vacation before, and I guess I went that day more out of curiosity than any sense of religious conviction, I'm sorry to say. As a matter of fact, during this trip to Jamaica, any religious convictions that I was holding on to had started to wane. It was partly because of my upbringing and former religious experiences. Something had happened to me during this trip to Jamaica in July of 2001 that has changed my total religious perspective forever. It was my spiritual awakening.

Being her last child and growing up very close to my mother, I was always sort of spiritually inclined. I don't remember ever seeing either of my parents going to church when I was a child, but my mother always had this spiritual air about her that was more than just a woman's intuition or a sixth sense. I will never forget this particular incident when my older brother, Barrie, went on a bicycle trip across the island with some of his friends from school. It was not the first time he had gone on one of these trips, but my mom was becoming increasingly worried. They had always left very early in the morning, and as the day progressed, my mom kept saying something was wrong on this trip.

When it got dark and my brother didn't come home, my mom went into a state of panic. She began to weep and even told a neighbor, Ms. Lucy, that she felt Barrie was in danger or might be hurt or killed. Ms. Lucy poured more kerosene on the fire when she told her that she felt the same way when her favorite grandson was killed on his way home from work a few years earlier. I remembered reading the entire book of Psalms and praying throughout the whole night with my mom. The next day, the news came when my brother came home. They had gone for a swim in one of the rivers, and one of the boys went out too far and drowned. Barrie was a good swimmer and tried to hold on to him, but he almost got swept away too and had to let go.

On July 9, 2005, my mother died. Her passing was significant because it ended an era in a life that had touched so many. Just like in Maverley where relatives and friends who left the country to find a better life in the city could find a lodging, her apartment at 1665 Fish Avenue in the Bronx was also a way station for many others who came from Jamaica and didn't have a place to stay in America. During her passing, she was surrounded by family members, and a niece was literally holding her hand when she took her last breath.

What was significant though was what happened immediately after her passing. Barrie had stepped outside into the courtyard of the apartment complex to smoke a cigarette. As he started to light up, he heard this screeching sound from a bird and thought for a moment the bird was injured and must be in some sort of distress. However, as he took away his attention from the bird and was about to light up, the bird flew over to him and knocked the cigarette from his hand. I have to tell you, my brother Barrie is not the kind of person to make up stories, and he related this incident only a few minutes after it happened when we walked over to the undertaker a couple blocks from the house. The undertaker, a young woman, overheard him and said, "She is definitely trying to tell you something." Some of you reading may consider this unbelievable or a lot of hype, but those of you who have a connection with the spirit of the ancestors (like my mother) will not.

Technically, I wasn't born a Seventh-day Adventist, but my mom told me her landlady was a Seventh-day Adventist and that when I was a few months old and it was time for me to be dedicated to the Lord, they took me to her church where I was blessed by the elders as the Seventh-day Adventist Church does not believe in christening or baptizing babies. When I met my beautiful wife, who was born in a Seventh-day Adventist family, my mom loved her so much and told me she knew I was going to marry that girl.

After leaving the church, I went back to the house and sat in the shop and talked with Papa for a little while. A few customers came in to buy bread and sugar and other items, but a lot of the young people came to buy bulla cake, peanut butter sandwiches. *That must taste very interesting,* I thought. I asked Papa if this was his special recipe, but he said this was what the young people were asking for. I told him about Everald's stomachache in church, and he said, "Dat bwoy eat too much a dem green mangoes dat's why him belly hat him."

Papa said he was going to Christiana to pick up some supplies and closed the shop. I passed by Everald who was lying down in bed, still in his church clothes with his shoes on. I went upstairs, put on my Take 6 in my Walkman, and started to write in my journal. After a few minutes of writing, I noticed a late model GMC sport pickup pull up at the gate with two young men—one in his late twenties or early thirties and the other in his early twenties. They were dressed in jeans and T-shirt and looked kind of thuggish. I could tell they were not from around here and wondered what these "rude boys" wanted. They opened the gate and came up to the burglar bar at the veranda.

The eldest of the two spoke, "Is Mr. Leslie here?" "No," I replied and told them they could stop by later. He said they were coming all the way from Kingston, and I could detect a slight irritation in his voice that came over kind of subtle. I immediately decided from their lack of brashness that they were not bandits and realized I had been stereotyping them much the same way I had been stereotyped by my sister's neighbors in Washington Gardens. "OK. Wait just a minute. Let me get the key." I opened the gate to the burglar bar that encased the veranda and let them in. "Have a seat and make yourselves comfortable," I told them and then turned on the television.

They didn't appear to pose any threat (as my threat antenna didn't go up), and I suspected that they were just as leery about me as I was about them initially. "Would you like some water or something," I offered. "Thank you, but that's all right," the older of the two answered. The younger guy only smiled but didn't speak. I introduced myself and said I was Ms. Leslie's nephew from New York. He said his name was Derrick and that he was Mr. Leslie's grandnephew. Soon, the ice was broken, and we began to strike up a conversation. I told him Diana was also visiting from New York but that she had to take David back to Kingston to see a doctor. He said he had never met Diana but had always wanted to meet her and that he had always kept in touch with Papa.

He said he was a sign and graphic artist and was in business for himself, and I told him I was a parole officer and that I was really visiting to check out a school for my son.

"Where?"

"West Indies College High School."

"Oh, that's a good school."

Everald came upstairs while we were talking, still wearing his black pants he had worn to church, but he had changed into a purple-and-black shirt. I told him he was looking kind of handsome and must be going on a date. He said he was going to Pourus to "look for his madda" (visit his mom). Pourus was on the way to Kingston about five miles south of Christiana, and he had intended to make the entire trip by walking all the way. I was planning to go to Christiana to make some phone calls, and I told him to wait for me so we could ride a taxi to Christiana together.

Everald all dressed-up to go visit his mom in Porus

Papa had just arrived from Christiana and was coming through the gate. He recognized his visitors and greeted them. He didn't seem especially concerned about the ten-mile trip Everald was about to take on foot to Pourus and said, "Him walk go de all di time." I decided to give Everald two US dollars and told him to use it for carfare to get to Pourus. While Papa was talking to his grandnephews, I got my digital camera out, and we all took pictures of and with each other. I showed them the pictures we had just taken on the camera, and Derrick asked if I could send him copies when I got home. I told him if he had a computer, I could e-mail them to him, and he gave me his e-mail address on the back of his business card. He also gave me an extra business card for Diana and asked me to tell her to contact him, which I assured him I would do.

Derrick said he was ready to leave now and that he would give me a ride into Christiana and drop off Everald in Pourus on his way back to Kingston. We kept in touch by e-mail when I got back to New York, and in his last e-mail to me, he wrote that he was going to get married. I never heard from him again, and all the subsequent e-mails from me and Diana were returned and undeliverable. I was happy for him and was glad we were given the opportunity to meet each other. Although technically we weren't related, we became like a family, and I was sorry when I lost contact with him.

Snapshot with Derick visiting from Kingston

The Seventh Day

It was Sunday, and the morning was a bit foggy. After having my daily meditation and making a few entries in my journal, I decided to get up and prepare myself for the day ahead. I wasn't sure what time Vaughn was coming to pick me up, but I wanted to be ready just in case he came early. First, I went downstairs to the kitchen where I had some organic granola cereal that I had brought from New York for breakfast; then I went to take a shower.

The water was ice-cold. Although the daytime temperature could get to the eighties, the water temperature stayed pretty much frigid especially early in the morning. As I had done every day I was there, I just closed my eyes and braved it. In a matter of seconds, my body adjusted to the water temperature, and it became a very refreshing experience as always. After I got finished, I went back upstairs and put on some shorts, a T-shirt and my sandals.

Through the window, I could see people outside the street all dressed up and walking to church. I turned on the Take 6 CD in the boom, went and sat on the veranda, and continued to write in my journal. It was an enjoyable experience just sitting there writing; I was feeling so relaxed, and my mind was completely devoid of stress. I thought that if I ever wanted to be a writer, this would be the ideal place to be one. I was anticipating

Vaughn's arrival at anytime, but I was actually hoping that he would take his time as I wanted to continue savoring these few moments to myself.

Vaughn arrived a few minutes after eleven with his girlfriend and their four-year-old son. Although I was anticipating his arrival and was happy to see him and his family, I nevertheless felt a little reluctant to leave and wanted to continue writing in my journal. I hoped and prayed I would be able to regain the same peace and momentum when I sit back down to write again.

Vaughn on duty adjusting his glock

As it turned out, the adventure I had begun to experience from day 1 in Jamaica was not fleeting, and I discovered meeting up with Vaughn would be just turning the next page. Vaughn returned with Papa after going downstairs to the shop to greet him. I told Papa I would be back later and to lock the gate. I went and sat in the passenger seat beside Vaughn; then we drove off with his girlfriend and son who were waiting in the back seat.

Vaughn was nicknamed Maroon because of his dark complexion by the people in the community where he worked as a detective, and he was a very gentle soul, which was apparent in his relationship with his son. He would say to him, "How much does Daddy love you?" and Chad would reply with glee and excitement, "Like this," with his arm stretched wide-open and give his daddy a kiss. I couldn't help but feel a little jealous and wished I was as affectionate to my sons back home as he was to his little boy.

We were serenaded by Vaughn who loved to sing romantic favorites from singers like Dean Martin, Frank Sinatra, Nat King Cole, Tom Jones, and the like. I remembered when I was a kid, these were the songs they used to play on RJR Sunday evenings after all the religious programs. I joined in the singing with Vaughn, trying to harmonize with his voice as we continued on our trip to St. Elizabeth where Vaughn lived and was stationed as a detective. I had few happier times in my life. God, this was wonderful.

About halfway to where we were headed, we stopped at a fruit stand, which had a variety of tropical fruits from the island. There were mangoes, sugarcanes, bananas, jelly coconuts, guinepes, neseberries, and more to choose from. Vaughn ordered jelly coconuts for everyone, and using his machete, the man chopped the head of the coconuts down to just where you could see the white meat and stuck a straw in them, and we drank the most refreshing drink one could imagine. After drinking the coconut water, he split the coconut in two, then made a spoon from the husk covering the coconut shell for us to eat the jelly inside. *Mmm*, it just melted in your mouth. While we were there, many other cars pulled up the road; business was good for the vendor with this fruit stand on the side of the road.

Breathtaking view of the sea on the road to St. Elizabeth

When we pulled off again, it didn't seem to take too long to reach Nain, the village in St. Elizabeth where Vaughn worked and where everyone called him Maroon. As we continued driving through the town, I noticed many of the people were having European features and were very fair skinned. Their noses were straight, and some of them had blue or green eyes with straight or curly hair. There were also dark-skinned, more African-looking people, but I couldn't tell who was the majority. Vaughn must have noticed me looking at everyone and said, "Dave, the people down 'ere light, but dem dark you see." I laughed at his unintentional contradiction in terms, but I knew exactly what he was saying. "Dem no joke fi tell you 'bout yu rass if yu cross them." (They will curse you out in a minute if you make them mad.)

I knew that most fair-skinned Jamaicans had a background in St. Elizabeth, but I didn't know the real history behind it. I remembered being told they were of German descent and just assumed that they had fled Germany during the time of Hitler's Nazi regime. But it didn't seem to make much sense because too many of them had Irish names like Riley, Kelly, and Murphy.

One day during the summer, I went to Home Depot in New Rochelle to buy some flowers to plant in my garden at home. There was this woman who was standing near me, looking at some seeds I was thinking of purchasing. She was white, probably in her late fifties, and looked Irish. I thought I would strike up a conversation and ask her about the different seeds it looked like we were both interested in. I was surprised when she answered back in a Jamaican accent. Before we discussed anything about gardening, I asked her which part of Jamaica she was from, and she said (you guessed it) St. Elizabeth. She said her name was Kathleen Reagan and that her grandparents were from Ireland.

I had a similar experience that happened to me when I was going to nursing school. I was doing my psychiatric rotation, and I was paired up with one of my classmates who happened to be of Irish descent. We were assigned to the same patients and were given an elderly patient who was a nun diagnosed with manic depression. When we went to see the patient, she was obviously in the manic phase of her disease, and we were both taken slightly aback by her incessant talking. She was dressed very casual for a nun, wearing only shorts and a blouse and with nothing on her head. As we approached her, the patient looked at us and said, "What happened? You're afraid of me because you think I'm a mad woman."

She was a sweet little old lady, and we told her we weren't afraid of her. We were able to engage her in some therapeutic conversation and got her to express her feelings while telling us more about herself. One of the things she told us was that she was dressed this way because the pope had told the nuns they should "get out of the habit." It was obvious to me while she was speaking that she was Jamaican, but Maureen, my Irish classmate, insisted that she was definitely Irish. We wagered a bet and discovered we were both right; our patient was born in Ireland but went to Jamaica as a young Catholic nun and never left there again until going to America some forty years later.

It was time for me to find out where these fair-skinned people who lived in St. Elizabeth really came from, and there was no better time to find out than while I was there. Who was better to ask than Vaughn who was educated in Jamaica and have been working in St. Elizabeth for the past several years? What he told me was that there was a shipwreck off the coast of St. Elizabeth and that the people on the ship came ashore and decided to settle there. That was all he told me, and although I had more questions I wanted to ask, such as where was the ship sailing from and when did the shipwreck occur, I decided to defer them until another time as Vaughn appeared to be a bit preoccupied.

We turned off the main road unto a dirt road leading into the mountains. After about half a mile, we stopped at a little wooden hut that was brightly painted in yellow, green, and red and a sign that bar on the front. This was a surprise as I had no idea where he was taking me when he had picked me up, and I perceived this was going to be his little side business to help supplement his government salary as a detective.

Behind the counter, there was a refrigerator and racks of Red Stripe beer, Heineken, and plenty of rum and other types of liquors. In the customer area, there were two arcade machines and some wooden stools next to the counter. Desrene got behind the counter and started to clean up while Vaughn and I messed around with the arcades to try to get them to work.

The outside area was open with several homes scattered about the hilly terrain. I noticed only a few onion and scallion farms around and concluded the people weren't too much into farming in these parts. A man and a woman soon pulled up outside in a late model pickup truck. They were fair-skinned and about Vaughn's age, which made them in their early thirties. They greeted me before Vaughn introduced me to them, and they appeared pleasant and helpful as they started to help fix up the bar while discussing business with Vaughn.

While we were cleaning and trying to set things up in the bar, two young men from the neighborhood stopped by and ordered Red Stripes. They were lively and jovial and asked Desrene if she was the barmaid. "No man, she's mi baby mother," Vaughn answered as an older man walked in and ordered another beer. He joined in the conversation as if they all knew each other and said Desrene (who was very brown-skinned) was the right color. While continuing to do his work and the men drank their Red Stripe beer, Vaughn said, "Don't worry. I'll get you a nice barmaid." The older man replied, "You need a brown gal fo' wo'k ya so" (you need a brown girl to work here). "Or a cooly gal" (or an Indian girl), continued one of the young men. Vaughn smiled as everyone chuckled.

I wondered if it was the alcohol speaking or were these men a little "color stricken" as some Jamaicans like to say. Using that term was more appropriate than "prejudice" because most of these light or brown-skinned people were really mulattos. Having lived in Jamaica for the first fourteen years of my life, I remembered enough to know that the statements that were made by those drunken men were most likely due to a combination of the alcohol they were consuming and how they really felt.

From within my own family, I became aware at an early age how important "colorism" is in Jamaican society. My paternal grandmother, whom everyone called Mother, was from St. Elizabeth and was very fair skinned as was my father, who was called Son and his two sisters, Sissy (Aunt Sis) and Violet, whom everyone called Nurse because she was a midwife. They lived in a nice area in Half Way Tree, St. Andrew, and had a live-in maid. I never knew Father, my paternal grandfather, who died before I was born but who I know my mom loved and adored. She always described him as being a good and gentle man and said that my dad was just like him. To all intents and purposes, she accused them of contributing to his demise, indicating that they didn't take good care of him while he was sick because he was black.

Even though I was allowed to and I frequently visit my father's side of the family, my mother kept a comfortable distance from Mother, Sissy, and Nurse and, from my recollection, never ever visited them in Half Way Tree. Nurse was already living in America by way of England before I was born, and I technically only knew her from pictures and her presents, which was sent from her monthly and, sometimes, biweekly support to the home in Half Way Tree. I also had an older sister, Lyn, my father's first child who I didn't know personally either. She was studying to be a nurse in England, and I only knew her from photographs.

My mother often talked about the physical and verbal abuse Lyn faced at the hands of Sissy and Nurse and the experience my father also had to endure as the youngest child and only boy. She said they treated him like Cinderella and that it was no wonder he married a dark-skinned woman like her. I could remember Aunt Sis coming up to Maverley a couple times and being treated with the greatest respect by my mom, but not soon after she left, my mom would cuss and say, "The three of dem think dem white." As a youngster, I couldn't understand why this was happening because I loved everyone in my family.

After I came to America, it wasn't colorism anymore but racism I had to learn about. It took me a while to learn what racism was really about. Yes, I had heard about what was happening in the South and the assassination of Dr. Martin Luther King Jr. but didn't personally feel affected by it. Being from a third world and majority black country, I was told and felt I could grow up to be whatever I wanted to be. Then after moving to New York, it just seemed strange how everybody was afraid of each other based on race. Like the time I was at Macy's in White Plains when this white lady saw me and grabbed her pocketbook off the counter, tightly clutching it under her arms as if I was about to rob her (even now this continues to happen) or the racial profiling by the police who will stop you if you're driving through a white neighborhood or the college professor I overheard making disparaging remarks about blacks with another white student, and when I confronted him, he told me, "You're not black. You're Jamaican," the right-winged radio stations, and so on.

A few years ago, I visited some relatives across the Atlantic in Birmingham, England. Two of my aunts from my mother's side had left Jamaica and had gone to live there from during the sixties, and I wanted to see them again and meet my cousins. I had encouraged my mom and dad to make the trip a few years before, and they came back quite hyped with a lot of stories and adventures they had experienced while they were there. They said everyone there wanted to meet me too and that I should consider taking a trip over there.

I had always wanted go to England, so it didn't require much convincing for me to make up my mind. It was around 1987 and I had completed college and was now working in a nice job as a warrant officer for the New York City Department of Probation. I was single and unattached, and it seemed like just the right time for me to make this trip. I flew out of Newark airport on a direct flight to Heathrow Airport on Virgin Atlantic Airways.

Although I had taken a few reading materials and my Sony Walkman, this six-hour flight could have gotten a little boring were it not for the beautiful flight attendants who appeared willing to cater to my every need and were just terrific in getting me anything I needed to make my flight comfortable. Their English accents over the plane's PA system sounded like nightingales and made me feel like I was already on English turf. The video monitor the airline provided at every seat was like icing on the cake; it was sweet.

I arrived at Heathrow Airport early the next morning and was surprised to find Othniel and Uncle Dickie, my aunts' husbands, waiting for me. I had not made any arrangements with them to pick me up and had planned to take the coach to Birmingham. So they were actually like a godsend as it was a long way to Birmingham, and I was feeling very tired and weary from the flight.

As we drove off on the left side of the road in Othniel's little Ford Escort with its right steering wheel, I noticed how nice the weather was—it was bright and sunny, the sky was blue with scattered white clouds floating high above, and the temperature felt in the low seventies and was comfortable. There was no London fog or drizzling rain I had always heard about London and thought I might experience. During our three-hour drive to Birmingham, we only stopped once at a service station for petrol (English for gas) where it was sold in liters. The English had gone totally metric, and everything was being measured in meters, liters, centigrade, etc. Even the English pound was now based on one hundred pence and not twelve pence equals one shilling and twenty-one shillings equals one pound as I was taught in school in Jamaica when it was under the English system.

My aunt Dell and Othniel lived in a nice three-bedroom house in the Chemsley Wood section of Birmingham. When I arrived, Chris and Tyrone, my cousins, were not there. I was told Chris, the eldest, stayed back and forth at his girlfriend's and only came home sometimes, while Tyrone had his own place and visited once in a while. I called Aunt Ven to let her know I had arrived safely and that I would be coming over to see her soon, which would be the following day. I stayed at Aunt Dell's the first night and slept in Tyrone's room, feeling bored out of my wits. They only had one television set and that was downstairs in the drawing room. English people were not into television that much, and I only had a little clock radio next to the bed with only stations from the BBC. Luckily, I had my Walkman and some reading materials I had brought with me.

Chris showed up the next day, and we hit it off like long lost cousins although it was the first time we actually met each other. Everyone, except his parents, called him Garfield (I thought because of his droopy eyes like Garfield the Cat), but it was actually his middle name. He was also a collector of little artifacts of Garfield the Cat and said he did so just for fun. Chris was twenty-three and thickly built, his complexion was dark brown, and he was around five feet nine. He was very easygoing and laughed out a lot in a very high-pitched *ha ayee* almost every five seconds, like everything I said was funny (maybe it was my Yankee accent).

I met up with my other cousins—Paul, Paulette, and David—when I went over to Ward End on the other side of town to see Aunt Ven. We bonded immediately with each of my younger cousins trying to compete for my attention. Paul, the oldest, was around eighteen and bore a slight resemblance to Chris (one could tell they were family), while David, the youngest, was tall, dark, and lanky. Paulette was petite and was a shade or two lighter than her brothers. I didn't realize that I was expected to spend the night until I got up to say good night and was getting ready to leave with Chris. Aunt Ven was visibly upset and implied that I already stayed two days with Aunt Dell and I didn't even come prepared to spend a few days with her (or something to that effect). Chris gave out one of his loud "ha haws," and we both knew what that meant: I was spending the night. They treated me like royalty and practically rolled out the red carpet.

The culture in Birmingham was totally unique and different from that in New York. I observed that white and black kids hang out together and that their favorite hangout was at the pub. Even underaged kids were allowed to hang out at the pub where everyone would socialize—chat, play pool or video games, listen to music, dance, kiss, and do whatever young people are allowed when at the pub. I could tell that Paulette was a little sheltered because a couple of times when she tried to introduce me as her cousin, her friends laughed and said, "Yeah, sure."

I was taken all over Birmingham and even hang out in London with Chris and one of his friends. I was introduced to a lot of people—my aunts' neighbors or friends of my cousins—as my nephew from America or my cousin from America. Everyone I met made me feel special, and their responses to my introduction were not only a sincere "How do you do?" but a short and pleasant conversation about some happenings in America and always ended with "I hope you enjoy your holiday here."

One Saturday night after the club where we were partying in Birmingham closed, Chris and I were heading back home. Both decks of the double-decker bus we were traveling in were packed with a bunch of other young people. No one was really rowdy, but everyone was chatting and having a good time when all of a sudden, from the back of the lower deck where we were seated, I heard, "Niggers, niggers." My muscles tensed as I looked back at the lone white youth who was shouting out those forbidden words every black man in America had learned to hate.

I looked around at all the other black youths who were on the bus and wondered why everyone kept laughing and talking even with other white youths. I felt like shouting, "Didn't you hear! The man called us niggers. Aren't you going to let us kick his ass?" Then I looked at Chris who had a smile on his face and who undoubtedly must have felt my rage. He rested his hand firmly on my shoulder as if to hold me down in my seat and simply said, "Relax, man. He's under his waters." My tension eased, and I just thought to myself, *Truly, I am not in America.*

Me and Chris on my tip to Birmingham, England

Vaughn borrowed his friend's pickup truck and left them in the bar, still cleaning and fixing up with Desrene and told me to come with him to pick up another arcade. He explained to me, as we were driving away, that arcades bring in a lot of money and that one of the arcades in his bar was actually loaned to him by the owner of the pickup and that he had to return it. We drove down the hill and back onto the main road, traveled about a quarter of a mile, then turned up another hill in the opposite direction from where his bar was located.

The road we were traveling on up the hill was paved with nicer, more expensive homes scattered sporadically on either side. We passed a plantation with a For Sale sign on it, and Vaughn told me that Mannings University was in this direction and that we were in a very well-to-do area. We drove for a couple more miles to get to our destination, which was another bar. Vaughn went inside and asked the two young men sitting at the counter to help get an arcade from inside the bar and into the truck.

It was barely past noon, and the two young men already seemed well on their way to getting drunk. They were friendly and said to Vaughn that he looked like the police. Vaughn smiled without saying anything. They looked at me who was dressed up kind of like a tourist in shorts and T-shirt and said that I too looked like a policeman. Unlike Vaughn, I denied it to which they quickly agreed and said that I sound foreign. This surprised me because I thought I was speaking in the purest patois I knew how.

Vaughn thanked them for their help and told the barmaid to give them a couple of Red Stripes on him. We left, and when we returned to Vaughn's bar, we found the other two men when we had left still there, pretty much intoxicated and dancing and singing to themselves. I really fell in love with St. Elizabeth—it's people and their idiosyncrasies. I will always have fond memories of my adventures in this beautiful parish that has forever been etched in my heart.

This the is Vaughn's Bar in St. Elizabeth

I returned to Craig Head after leaving St. Elizabeth, anticipating my return to America and thinking how much my life would be different when I get home. Everything that happened during my stay from the first night up to this point, I cannot just write off as pure coincidence. I knew I had to get to Jamaica at this time for precisely this experience. Oh god, I wish it didn't have to end, and I didn't have to return home. But I made up my mind (and knew) that from now on, how I view life on this planet would never be the same. It seemed as if at the time of my birth, I started in a circle, and everything that happened to me in life during my journey around this circle was in preparation for what I had to receive during this trip to Jamaica.

I can tell you right now that as a direct result of this experience, I now know, more than ever, who I am and what I was placed on this earth for. My out-of-body experience on my second day on the island is something that I still don't understand and still continues to baffle me. You can understand when I tell you I was destined to make this trip to Jamaica at this particular time with Diana and her boys.

I went home to the Bronx and resumed my life with my family and continued to work and go to church on Sabbath as I did before, but there was a recognition I was continuing on my spiritual journey that got ignited in Jamaica. Yes, I did find myself following the same pattern I had left behind before the trip, but I also found that I was yearning to find more of my true spiritual self. I now fully realized that God was my creator and not a creature and how manipulative organized religions are. Going to church now was more out of habit than out of any defined belief. I listened to the preacher and, in my heart, was begging him to please tell me something new. Nothing had changed; all I was getting was a lot of theatrics and the same recycled sermons I've been hearing for years, and my soul was not being ministered to. It appeared very obvious to me how money was at the crux of the church's purpose, and everything else was secondary. Every Sabbath, they kept referring to the Bible passage found in Malachi 3:8-9 which says,

> Will a man rob God?
> Yet you have robbed me!
> But you say,
> "In what way have we robbed You?"
> In tithes and offerings.

Then verse 9 continues,

> You are cursed with a curse,
> For you have robbed Me.

I find it so contradictory that a loving God who sent his son to die for the sins of so many that "no one should perish, but have everlasting life" (John 3:16, KJV) would send someone on a fixed income straight to hell if they can't afford it. I remember this deacon one Sabbath at church boastfully telling me he double tithed, which I interpreted would entitle him to a double portion of the divine's blessing. There is nothing wrong with supporting the church financially if you are able to do so; the church could not survive without money, but what I take issue with is the contingency upon one's giving and doing "good works" based on the expectation of receiving God's blessings and getting a one-way ticket to heaven. Where then is the virtue? The church ought to stop using shame and guilt to get people to support it. The church would flourish beyond measures and people would lend more financial support if they believed it was truly fulfilling God's commission in the world. If they were truly following Jesus's example, who was the most altruistic person that ever lived, it would be apparent that giving without the thought of receiving is what it is all about.

It is not the church I have a problem with but the system of leadership. I love the church and believe the church (not just our church) and most religious institutions serve a major purpose in society. Personally, I have found that it gave me a balance, another way of looking at life, and the discovery of my own spiritual nature. Without going to church, I'm not sure I would be the spiritual being I profess to be. I guess that is why I continue to go to church and why I send my children to religious institutions for their education and not because it has anything to do with salvation. I will not be coerced with the threat of eternal damnation and go against my spiritual guidance system.

It's a historical fact that Jesus did walk this earth and his life was, undoubtedly, an example of how mankind should live. It is plain he didn't own anything or even had a place of his own to live, "Foxes have dens, and birds in the sky have nests, but the Son of Man has no place to lay his head" (Matthew 8:20, NET). Yet while he was alive, he gave away more than any other person in history down to his very life. I don't cherish the idea of judging anyone based on their beliefs or religion, but I don't see much difference between the religious leaders of today from the ones Jesus pointed to so much in the scriptures.

Although so learned and educated, the religious leaders felt so threatened by Jesus's way of life and his love for his fellowman that they eventually conspired and had him executed. After they brought him the prostitute to be stoned in John 8:10 and he said anyone without sin should throw the first stone and looked around and didn't see anybody, he said to the woman, "Where did all your accusers go?" When she said they left, he said to her, "Well, I don't condemn you either." I truly believe (and this is my personal opinion) that if it was possible for Jesus to return today and if he didn't look the way they expected him to look, or didn't say the things they expected him to say, they would try to discredit him and conspire to put him to death all over again.

Breath of Life

There is a sister in my church who I admire immeasurably and whose example I think mirrors Jesus's life more than any other church member, deacon, elder, or pastor for that matter. I'll call her Sister V. She is everybody's friend, and as long as I've been attending that church, I have never seen her gossip or say anything disparaging against anyone in the church. Whenever something needs to be done in the church and there is nobody to do it, you can always count on Sister V to do it. Some of the positions she has held in church are the following: director of personal ministries, women's ministries, health ministries, children's ministries, church clerk, deaconess, and usher. As I write, she is currently holding dual posts as sabbath school director and director of the Pathfinders Club. While I've seen others get plaques and is duly recognized by the church, I have never seen Sister V get even so much as a bouquet of flowers. She faithfully does all this while being a mother and holding down two jobs as a nurse.

One day after service, I was downstairs with everyone, having lunch in the church's cafeteria. A few tables away from where I was eating, I heard some commotion and happened to notice a crowd gather around someone who had collapsed around the lunch table. As a nurse, I wondered what was happening and quickly went to see how I could help. It appeared to be too late when I got there because an elder brother had just had a heart attack. He had no pulse, he was not breathing, and his eyes were open and fixated. Sister V quickly lowered him to the floor and started to perform CPR.

Another nurse and I were by her side but was not thinking he was going to pull through. After doing several chest compressions, I heard her say, "Let me give him two breaths," and then blew two puffs of air in the brother's mouth. She was about to start the compressions again when I noticed the brother blink. "He has a pulse!" I shouted after feeling his radial pulse on his right hand. The brother was taken to the hospital and is still alive today over a year later thanks to Sister V. She is probably one of the reasons why I still attend church and my faith has not wavered too far.

My trip to Jamaica was not only adventurous but also reminded me how homesick I was when I first came to America. The only picture I had in my mind of America prior to going there was what I had seen on the movies and on the television. At fourteen, I was not thinking about the racism and oppression everyone knew existed in America; instead, I chose to believe the beautiful images and good things I'd seen and heard people say about America. Why then would so many people in Jamaica, including people in my family, want to go there? It was the richest country in the world, and the streets were paved with gold. I thought black people there were better off than black people in Jamaica and would welcome me with open arms because we are all family.

I had idolized some of the few blacks I had seen on television like Sidney Portier, Diane Carol, and Bill Cosby and really believed this was actually how black people really lived in America. I was leaving paradise, but I was going to the closest place next to heaven was what I thought. There was no welcome mat when I arrived at John F. Kennedy International Airport in Queens, but I was still happy to be in America up to that point. Things got even better after we were picked up at the airport in a Pontiac Lemans. This was the biggest and prettiest car I'd ever seen and driven in all my life. As a matter of fact, all the cars I saw were huge; I didn't see any Austin Cambriges or Minny Minors. The man who picked us up was Jamaican and was a further poof to me of how successful blacks were in America.

We left JFK and traveled on the highway and across this huge bridge with hundreds of cars and trucks beside, in front, and behind us. Some of the trucks were so huge that when they passed us, we felt the car we were in sway a little. My imagination started to get the best of me, *Oh my gosh, what is this? How can this bridge support all these cars and trucks? And we've been on it for miles already. What would happen if a piece of the bridge gave way and our car fell into the water? I can't even swim.* Before I could finish thinking about falling hundreds of feet below and into the water and see all my life flash in front of me before drowning, we arrived at a booth near the end of the bridge where our driver had to give a woman dressed in a brown uniform some money before she would let us go through. *Whew!* I was glad to cross over this bridge and thought how long have people been driving over this bridge and wondered if what I was thinking had ever happened.

OK. So now I'm in America, and reality started to kick in: the streets aren't paved with gold. The driver did not know his way around the Bronx that well and only knew how to get to Ms. Burke's building in the South Bronx. As we drove through the South Bronx, I noticed that a lot of the buildings were boarded up and looked abandoned. Most of them appeared to have been destroyed by fire, and even the occupied buildings looked like they had seen better days. They were dark and dreary, and the streets were dirty with garbage, not much different than on Spanish Town Road next to Coronation Market in Kingston. And there weren't any houses, just buildings. We passed this bodega, and I saw this young man standing outside the door without a shirt on. Oh my gosh, I'm having a nightmare, and I'm not really in America. This place is impoverished (I wasn't familiar with the term "ghetto" at that time).

We were dropped off at 775 Jennings Street where Ms. Burke lived. She pressed a button next to the entrance of the building and then someone answered, "Who is it?" Ms. Burke said, "Buzz me in," and when a buzzer went off, she pushed the door open, and we all went inside the building. The driver helped us take our grips (suitcases) upstairs to the third floor where she lived, but we had to wait several minutes until the young lady inside (her niece) could find the key to one of the three locks that was on the door.

I never thought I would be able to ever smile again because at that moment, I went into a state of depression. They had taken me out of paradise and brought me to hell. Later, my dad came to pick up my mother and me to take us home. It was a summer evening, and there was still a little daylight left. Dad was very happy to see us, but I could tell he was not the same gentle soul I had as a father in Jamaica. He appeared gruff, and his speech and mannerism were different. Later, I found out why he was that way. New York was the "Land of the Gruffs." Everyone seemed to be like that. I wondered how long it was going to take me to become a gruff. I told myself I wasn't going to be here long enough to find out because I was going to go back to Jamaica. My strategy was to cry and whine every day so there would be no doubt in anybody's mind how unhappy I was, and they would send me home.

I didn't know where my father was taking us until the taxi dropped us off at this brown door on the sidewalk of 1660 Nelson Avenue in the West Bronx. My heart sank even deeper when he opened the door. He was the building superintendent, and there were shovels, garbage cans, and pieces of furniture scattered here and there in the living room. There were two bedrooms: one to the right and another to the left. The one to the left was the master bedroom (if you could call it that) and faced the sidewalk. It also opened up into the kitchen, which opened up into the basement. My dad told me to sleep in the bedroom to the right, which had a little bed in it. I threw my stuff on the floor next to the door and just lay on my back across the bed with my feet on the floor and with my shoes still on. Next thing I know, I was back in Jamaica. Pity I had to wake up.

Welcoming Committee

I woke up the next morning, still lying across the bed with my feet on the floor. The main entrance of the building was around the corner on Nelson, and there was another walk-in apartment right next door to us on West 174th Street. Dad had gone upstairs to work in one of the apartments. *Bam, bam, bam.* Somebody was knocking at our front door. It was my personal welcoming committee from next door that consisted of this teenage girl around my age and her younger sister and brother. Dad had apparently told them before that I would be coming and had told them that I had arrived when he passed them on his way going into the building. Their family had moved from South Carolina, and they looked and sound real country.

When I opened the door, I could tell they were very excited to see me, and the younger sister just shouted, "Oh, he's so purty!" I just stood there without saying anything and did something that I regret until this day: I slammed the door on their faces without speaking a word to them. Except for being a little depressed from being homesick, I don't know who I thought I was because even when I saw them again after that, I never spoke to them and truly am sorry. They were always playing by themselves because the other kids did not speak to them either.

Ms. Singleton was a neighbor from across the street and a friend of my father. She had a daughter named Susie, and they stopped by to see us that afternoon. Susie was much taller than me but was one year younger. I didn't think her face was all that cute, but she dressed nice with jeans and white sneakers. Ms. Singleton was tall and dark-skinned and spoke loud and crusty like a man. She had the persona of someone who would cuss you out in a minute if you got on her wrong side. Susie said she was going shopping with her mother.

"Where?" I asked.

"Menhaaden."

"Men what?"

She pointed to a store flier she was carrying. "Oh, Man-hat-tan," I said pronouncing it phonetically.

"No, it's Men-haa-den," she said again this time slowly. Before they left, Ms. Singleton had invited us over to her place for dinner the following week.

Chick Fest

I grew up a very picky eater and did not eat any kind of meat except beef, mutton, or salt (cod) fish. Ms. Wong was our neighbor in Jamaica and was of Chinese ancestry. They used to raise pigs and pigeons, and occasionally, they would butcher one of these animals when I was hanging out at their place. They used to call me a "ginal" because I would pretend I heard Mom calling me and said I had to go. At our place, we used to raise chicken. We called them fowls and gave each one of them names, and they were just like another pet to me like our dog or cat. I was very young when I first witnessed them chop off the head of one of the fowls. It was a very traumatic experience for a five—or six-year-old to watch as the fowl ran several yards without its head and faltered before it was caught again, plucked, and cooked for Sunday dinner. I don't remember if I had ever eaten a chicken before that happened, but I knew I would never eat that fowl or any chicken again, period.

The day had come, and it was time for us to go over to Ms. Singleton's for dinner. Susie was now being referred to as my girlfriend by her mother. I wasn't sure if she was saying it generically as in Susie is a girl and she is my friend or we were girlfriend and boyfriend. I had a feeling it was the latter as Susie did not appear to be very popular with the other guys on the block. When we arrived at their apartment, Ms. Singleton said to Susie, "You and your boyfriend go into the living room." Susie tried to be entertaining by asking me about what are some of the things I liked, places I wanted to visit, etc. She became a little upset with me because with every answer I gave her, I started by saying, "In Jamaica I did this or that," and painted a very beautiful picture of Jamaica with my words. At one point, she said to me, "If Jamaica is so beautiful, why did y'all come here?" This was more of an angry rhetorical response than a question.

It was time to eat, and guess what was being served for dinner? You guessed it. Chicken. I was sitting beside Susie and pushed away the plate of chicken, mashed potato, and string beans that her mother had served me. All eyes were upon me, and I could see the embarrassment on my mother's face. I didn't have to say anything and could feel Susie staring at me more than anyone else. As I slowly pulled back the plate toward me, I felt a sigh of relief from everyone. My behavior did not go unnoticed, which caused Ms. Singleton to remark, "Everybody eats chicken in America." I ate it as polite conversation around another topic continued between my parents and Ms. Singleton.

Ms. Singleton also became a very good friend of my mother and was very kind to me. She was always taking me and Susie somewhere. I remember her taking us to the Turtle Back Zoo and to the Palisades Amusement Park in New Jersey. When it was time to go to school, she accompanied my mom and me and helped us during the registration process. She even took me shopping for school supplies and bought me a fall jacket. Her love and kindness went a long way to help alleviate some of my homesickness but not totally. I had a very verbose personality and didn't really have any problems making friends and fitting in at school. I volunteered to be a school monitor and wrote articles for my high school paper, *The Taft Review*.

Me at age 15 feeling very homesick at this particular time

One summer day, about a year after graduating from high school, I was standing outside my door on the sidewalk and ran into this Jamaican guy I knew from school. Michael Laings was Mr. Personality, and everybody knew him at Taft High School. He was wearing a Rastafarian knitted cap with a few of the dreads sticking out from the back.

"Hey, what's up, Heron?"

"Nothing much, man. What's up with you?"

"Everything irie. Just coming from checking some brethren down the street and heading back to the crib."

We spoke for a little while and, before he walked off, gave me the address for the crib.

"The man must come check me, seen?"

"Yeah man, One day."

"All right, little more."

Michael was a couple of years older than me and one class ahead of me in school, so we weren't really that close, and I only know him because he was a Yardie.

Rasta Man's Vibrations

By now, I was in the country for a few years already, had graduated from high school, and had completed a year of college. This was the seventies, and there were hippies, bell-bottoms, Jimi Hendrix, the Beatles, afros, and dashikis. Yes, and then there were the Rastafarians and Bob Marley's music was just making its way on the scene. The lyrics to his songs were so relevant and stirred up so much feelings inside me that sometimes I felt like I would cry. Cry because his music touched the deepest recesses of my soul. "Concrete Jungle," "Rebel Music," "Get Up, Stand Up," and "Duppy Conquerer" from his earlier albums were just genius; the man was an unwitting prophet. Whenever I hear any of his music, I never felt more connected and more proud to be a Yardie. His music had so much profound meaning, and even he himself was surprised how others interpreted his lyrics. My brother who lives in Windsor, Canada, told me that there was a group of mostly white kids (he's not sure what they're called, Marlyites maybe) who follow his music like a cult. Although some of them wear dreadlocks, they're not Rastafarians; it's all about the music.

I was still very unhappy about being uprooted from Jamaica and brought to live in New York, but as the years passed, I was more or less getting assimilated into American society. I related so much to his song, "Natty Dread," that I became homesick every time I hear it. Here are some of the lyrics that meant so much to me.

> Oh! Children don't forget your culture
> And don't stay here and gesture
> . . .

Then I walk over to first street,
And then I walk up the second street
. . .
Oh, Natty, Natty
21,000 miles away from home, yeah!
. . .
Oh, Natty, Natty
And that's a long way
For Natty to be from home
. . .
Natty Dread, Natty Dread now
Dreadlock Congo Bongo I.
Natty Deadlocks in a Babylon,
Oh, Roots, Natty Roots. Natty.

But now there was political upheaval in Jamaica as indicated by another one of his songs, "Rat Race," and paradise has never been the same since.

One day, I went to the crib to check out Michael. It was down the road from Taft on East 165th Street and Sheridan. He introduced me to some of his brethren—Mast' Hugh, Vino, and Mast' Hugh's younger brother, Fi, who was around my age. Everyone had dreadlocks except Mast' Hugh who appeared very articulate and was obviously the brain of the posse. The crib was his and was a hangout for the other dreads, including Michael, who everybody called Laings or Mikey Laings. Mast' Hugh was brown-skinned like me and about the same height. He didn't dress thuggish or act militantly but looked like a rude boy, which kind of overshadowed a pleasant demeanor. One could tell he was not somebody to be messed with.

Mast' Hugh was cool and rolled me a spliff. He asked me what college I went to and nodded when I told him that I went to John Jay. "Hey, isn't John Jay that law school?" he asked. "No, it's called John Jay College of Criminal Justice, but it's just a regular four-year college that offers courses in criminal justice or prelaw." He appeared to be very impressed, but out of the corner of my eyes, I could see the suspicious look on Dougbert's face who later told Mast' Hugh I looked like a "beast" (cop) or a spy. You see, the crib was an apartment where Mast' Hugh sold weed out of, and while I was there, several people had already stopped by to purchase nickel bags. Mast' Hugh himself told me what Dougbert had stated and said he knew I was cool and that Dougbert was only an ignoramus. I trusted him like I trusted Michael and knew he too would be an ally if I ever needed one.

I started to lock my hair, and soon, the crib became a regular hangout for me too. I went there mostly every day, and I used to enjoy getting into intellectual conversations with Michael and Mast' Hugh. In one of our discussions, Michael, who was unemployed and helped Mast' Hugh hustle weed, indicated he wouldn't go to college because they only brainwash you there to learn to work for the white man and that he was never going to work for the white man. Mast' Hugh's take on the subject was that it takes a wise man to make an honest million and a wise man to make a dishonest million and that this was how he was going to make his million. At least, he had his own hustle, and I respected him for that. Rastafarians were stereotyped as marijuana smokers and dealers, and in fact, smoking weed was part of their religious ritual. However, not all Rastafarians sold weed and many of them worked and or or attended school. Although he spoke and acted like a Rastafarian, Mast' Hugh chose not to have dreads because he was undocumented and wanted to stay under the radar of the police who was always stopping and harassing Rastafarians.

I eventually dropped out of school and was spending more time with the posse than I wanted to admit. I was now a full-fledged Rastafarian and began attending the Ethiopian Orthodox Church. Around the posse, I was known as Dahu (Swahili for

David); but when I got baptized at the church, I was given my Ethiopian name by the abba—Kinfe Mika'el, which meant "Wings of Saint Michael" and was called Kinfe by most of the brethren and Mika'el or Michael by some. At the church, I joined up with some dreads who had started a reggae band called the Sons of David and became one of the lead singers and the band's manager. We played gigs all over the place but mostly at college campuses.

The marijuana business was becoming quite lucrative for Mast' Hugh. He was not only selling nickel and dime bags anymore but dealing in weights—pounds of marijuana smuggled into the country from Jamaica—and was the supplier for most of the other weed dealers in the city. Because there was a lot of cash flow and merchandise at the crib, it had now become an armed fortress with everybody packing anything from .32s to .357 Magnums. When there was a knock on the door, it was usually Vino who tiptoed to the door with his weapon drawn, quietly slid the peephole cover open, and gave a hand wave indicating that the coast was clear. If the person standing outside the door was not recognized, he would raise his hand without the wave to alert everyone. All weapons would be drawn at this point, and any weed and money would be stashed in a makeshift hiding place under the floor. Mast' Hugh or Mikey would carefully go take a peep, and the door wouldn't be opened if the person was not known. Security was vital; they not only had to worry about the police but also stickups by other drug dealers.

Mast' Hugh had gotten married and had another apartment where his wife and their baby lived. He was a shrewd businessman, trusting no one and never left his weed or his money at the crib even with his brother who lived there. Most nights when he went home to his family, he would take his weed and money and, of course, his .32 with him. Sometimes, I would hitch a ride with him in the taxi if I was there when he was leaving, which was usually around two or three o'clock in the morning.

I will never forget this particular night, around two o'clock in the morning, when we left the crib and were trying to catch a cab to go home. We were walking on 165th Street heading west toward the Grand Concourse where it would be easier to find a taxi, and saw this woman walking a couple feet ahead of us. She looked like she was afraid we were going to attack her. She was periodically turning around to look at us and walking kind of fast. Suddenly, we noticed a police car at the corner of 165th and the Concourse about half a block from us. "Dahu, this woman is going to make these cops stop us, and I'm not going back to Jamaica," Mast' Hugh said to me. It would be too suspicious if we turned around and headed back because they had probably already spotted us. I didn't say anything but thought, *You're worried about going back to Jamaica. What about going to jail?* But I knew what he was saying—going to jail meant going back to Jamaica for him.

Before another thought could come into my head, I heard him say, "Dahu, anyhow they try to stop us, I'm going to blaze them up." *What! You're going to do what?* I thought. I didn't want to believe him, but I knew he was serious after I heard the click coming from his right-hand jacket pocket and realized he had cocked the trigger of his .32 in preparation to shoot. *Oh my god, what am I going to do?* was all I could think of at the moment. I tried not to act afraid, but I was sweating, and my heart was pounding as we continued walking toward the police. *Does this guy think he can kill New York's finest and get away with it? Don't want to go back to Jamaica. What about me? Do I deserve to spend the rest of my life in jail because you're crazy enough to kill a cop?*

When we reached the patrol car, the cops appeared preoccupied with something else, and the woman turned left on the Grand Concourse still walking hurriedly. We hailed a cab that was about to turn onto 165th Street and sped away in it. We didn't speak to each other until the cab dropped me off at my place, and he said, "I'll see you later." "Yeah, later," I said.

The crib eventually got busted, and Mast' Hugh was arrested. I'm sure it was a setup because he now had some competition from a lot of other people in the business who would benefit tremendously if they could get rid of him and steal his customers. This was a dog-eat-dog business. There must have been some kind of plea bargain that was made between him and the district attorney because a little while after his release, he moved to Florida. By this time, I'm sure he had received his green card through his wife, who was a legal resident, and there was no real danger of him being deported.

I started hanging out with Michael who had inspirations of becoming independent and doing his own thing. He started doing his own little hustle here and there and, eventually, got a crib. Except for Mikey, Fi, and me, the original posse had more or less broken up after Mast' Hugh's departure. Tony, Vino's cousin, started to hang with us. He was not a dread, half-Indian, and looked and acted like a pretty boy. There were girls galore, and baby mothers were springing up all over the place. Mikey started to do well in his own right by now, and I helped him find a store on Mount Eden Avenue near the train station to front as a record store. Mikey cut off his dreads and was looking more like a real businessman; he wore a jacket and bought a brand-new Monte Carlo.

Everybody started to drift, but Speng and I always kept in touch. He had lost his record store, and his ride was repossessed. He had gotten a new crib on College Avenue just a couple of blocks away from Taft where we attended high school, and I used to go over there sometimes to check him and burn some weed. His girlfriend was American and cute with a nice body and chocolate-brown complexion. A few times, I would go there when he wasn't home; and while waiting for him to arrive, she would whine and complain to me about how he was abusing her. At times, she would even show me where he hit her; and although I felt sorry for her, it was their business, and I didn't want to get involved. *Why was she complaining to me anyway, and what did she expect me to do about it? If you didn't like the way you were being treated, you had options, and I wasn't one of them,* I thought to myself. My loyalty was to my friend, and I just wish she would leave me alone.

If Mikey did not get back to his crib within a few minutes to about half an hour, I would usually leave because there were no cell phones to call him to see where he was. One day, he arrived just when I was about to leave. I could sense that he was not happy from the way he responded after I greeted him but didn't consider I was the problem. He began to act very suspicious although not directly accusing me of anything. I have seen him angry before, but this was the first time his anger was directed at me. I started thinking, *I just know he didn't believe I was doing anything with his girl.* He was cursing and swearing in Jamaican, "Blood claat, bumbo claat, rass claat," and his behavior was totally out of context toward me when suddenly, he pulled his .38 revolver from his waist. I wasn't scared nor did I feel intimidated if that was his intent because I know he would never hurt me. Yet what he did was one of the worst things that anyone had ever done to me in all my life. I have been threatened with a gun up close during my involvement with Mast' Hugh posse days, but Mikey took it a step further. Yes, right there in that apartment that day, someone who I considered to be my best friend pistol-whipped me like it was nobody's business.

I was hurt not so much from the incident that just took place, but more from someone I trusted and loved like a brother would even think of doing this to me. Years later, I was actually able to forgive him and felt some compassion in my heart toward him; but at that moment, there was nothing in my heart but hatred for him. I told him someday they are not only going to find him dead but also decomposed. He looked at me with sad, droopy eyes and said, "So that was what you were always wishing for me," as if that would justify what he just did. We both knew that would be the end of our friendship as I just hung my head down and walked out of the apartment.

I eventually moved on and started to identify more with the brethren from the Ethiopian Orthodox Church and my band. Although their belief and way of life was definitely based on the Rastafarian tradition, they were not all "natty dreads," did not all smoke weed, and there was no need for anybody to tote a gun. Our band leader, Gabre Maskel, who I adopted as a role model, was a graduate student at Boston College. I began to appreciate a different side of this Rasta philosophy that came from a more spiritual perspective.

I wanted to go back to school and began attending a technical school to become a medical lab technician. After completion of that course, I was accepted to do an internship in microbiology at the North Central Bronx Hospital. I got a job as a phlebotomy technician at Montefiore Medical Hospital where I went to the patients' room on the floor and drew blood from six to eight o'clock in the morning; then I went over next door to NCB Hospital to do my training from nine to five. While holding these two positions, I started going to night school at Mercy College where I majored in behavioral science with an emphasis in psychology and minor in community health.

As events turned out, soon after receiving by bachelors from Mercy College, I also completed my internship and received my medical technician license. However, I opted not to work as a lab technician and accepted a job as a mental health technician at North Central. This position seemed very timely that it required a bachelor's degree in my field and enabled me to work in collaboration with other disciplines (psychiatrists, psychologists, psychiatric social workers, and nurses) on a locked unit with patients having mental health issues.

After about six months of working on this job, I applied and was accepted at Columbia University in the City of New York to pursue a master's degree in social work. I left after one year into what was supposed to be a two-year program and began working as a probation officer in New York City. From there, I went to work for the state as a parole officer. During my transition from city probation to state parole, I found the love of my life, and we got married. We had our first son and named him Michael after my friend Mikey Laings. The rumor was that he had gotten killed after he was shot in the face. But one day while I was working in the office, a coworker told me a blind guy who said he was not a parolee was in the waiting area asking to see me. I asked if she wouldn't mind escorting him to my desk, and yes, it was Mikey.

Evadne modeling for me on our honeymoon in Grand Bahama

So I got the house in the suburbs, bought my BMWs, and was making a six-figure salary. I said "was" even though as I write this chapter this is my current situation. Yet I would be willing to give it all up to find my true purpose in life. I know I didn't take on this physical state and came into this world just to amass an enormous amount of material possessions. I am aware that they (money and material possessions) may come as collateral of living a successful life. But what does a successful life really mean? Does it mean working hard until you retire then surviving a few more years (usually on a pension and social security) until you die or amassing a tremendous amount of money and luxury but didn't live long enough to enjoy it? I don't think so. I feel I came here to be happy and to enjoy life to its fullest.

To me, money is like an instrument one must use for the basic necessities of life and then more. In today's society that's more than just food, shelter, clothing, but it also includes a telephone or computer for communication, some means of transportation or mobilization, and of course, health care. There is no way anyone can survive without these added necessities even if they are living in the poorest community. Hence, money must be spent for our basic survival. Then society tells us we need to have more, and we start to define ourselves by living in the biggest homes, driving the most expensive cars, wearing the nicest clothes, going on the most expensive vacations, and filling ourselves up with all sorts of entertainment. The more we get is the more we want, so we keep spinning around on a wheel like gerbils. We never feel satisfied because we can never have enough. The more we have, the happier we think we will be is what we believe until we either figure it out, or we don't.

> Do not accumulate for yourselves treasures on earth,
> where moth and rust destroy and where thieves break
> in and steal.... For where your treasure is, there your
> heart will be also. (Matthew 6:19 and 21, NET)

My wife recently went to her uncle's wedding in Toronto, Canada. He remarried after his wife of close to thirty years died of cancer. Her cancer was so aggressive that there was nothing much the doctors could do for her after the diagnosis. When my wife came back from Toronto, she described how big and beautiful their home was and how hard her uncle's wife had worked. "She had three jobs," she told me and that sometimes she didn't even come home for a couple of weeks, and then it would only be for a weekend. "She was such a nice lady," she added.

Working hard to accumulate material possessions doesn't bring happiness. In fact, it does just the opposite: it could rob you of precious time you could otherwise use to enjoy life and spend time with your family or stop you from finding your true passion in life to learn who you really are and passing it on as an example to your children. At the end when you look back, would you be happier saying, "Yes, I worked hard in life and accumulated a lot of possessions" or would it have been more preferable to say, "I am happy I had time to be with and provide for my family"? This is all subjective, of course, and I know some would say, "I'd rather have the money," believing it would help them contribute more to their family. I can empathize with that idea, but what would happen if after working so hard and getting all the money and all the possessions just to lose it all? Some may say it was worth it, and they would do it all again no matter what the cost.

Do you remember the rich young ruler in the Bible who came to Christ and said, "Teacher, what must I do to inherit eternal life?" And Jesus said to him, "Do not commit adultery, do not murder, do not steal, do not give false testimony, honor your father and mother." The man replied, "I have wholeheartedly obeyed all these laws since my youth." When Jesus heard this, he said to him, "One thing you still lack. Sell all that you have and give the money to the poor, and you will have treasures in heaven. Then come, follow me." But when the man heard this, he became very sad, for he was extremely wealthy. When Jesus noticed this, he said, "How hard it is for the rich to enter the kingdom of god!" (Luke 18:18-24, NET).

I don't want it to seem like I am bashing the rich or people who have become successful. It may be that in your situation, wealth is required, and you have handled success admiringly. But for most of us, life has been downright brutal in the quest to achieve more wealth and success. Hard work makes life difficult for most people and causes stress, which can lead to a disease and a shorter life span. Because our society has defined what it means to be successful, even if one has accomplished their goal and have achieved great financial success, it's only human nature that they're going to want to have more in order to keep up their status, which is no easy feat. If more of us would do an introspection and channel our thoughts into finding out what we are truly passionate about and not let the focus be on money, we would find that life was not meant to be hard or difficult, and there would be less stress and diseases.

A few chapters ago, I told you that I would be willing to give it all up: the pursuit of material attainment to find my true purpose in life. Ironically, a few weeks after writing that statement, I came home from work and, as I usually do, went in my den and sat in front of my desk to complete some notes from my job on the computer. Larnelle, my youngest son who had an after-school job about half a mile away, called and asked me to pick him up from work. My wife had just finished preparing dinner and wanted to know if she should dish it out or wait until I get back. I almost didn't make it back.

Cruising in fifth gear in my six-speed 335xi BMW coop on my way back home with Larnelle, we stayed in the right lane as we were going straight, and all left-lane traffic had to turn at the next intersection, which was about seventy-five yards away. It was twilight, and traffic was heavy because it was rush hour. Snow was on the ground from our first snowstorm the night before, but the streets were clean. This guy driving in the opposite direction in a huge suburban sports utility vehicle decided he wanted to make a left turn to enter the gas station we just happened to be passing at that moment. By the time I saw him, it was too late, and—*boom!*—we collided.

The airbags were inflated, and the windshield and driver-side window glass blew out. My car was totaled. I saw my whole life utterly flash before my eyes in an instant. I am convinced that if I was driving another car other than this sturdy German-engineered vehicle, I wouldn't be alive to tell about it. I was so upset about how this guy almost took us out, but honestly, I grieved more about losing my car. The firemen and the police on the scene were amazed at how Larnelle and I walked away without even a scratch from such a horrific accident. One of the firemen who heard me brooding about my car said to me, "You can replace a car, but you can't replace life or limb." That was a definite reality check for me.

Although I wished things hadn't worked or turned out the way it did, this accident could've been a blessing in disguise. Michael had bought a new 2010 Chevrolet Camaro and was just driving all over the place with his friends and was hardly ever at home. He was working at the Ritz-Carlton as a concierge and, at age 20, was making a good salary. However, like most young people his age, he was very irresponsible picking up parking tickets and even a couple moving violations that was sure to make my insurance rate go up. I started to wonder if I had done the right thing cosigning for him to get this car. He worked nights at the Ritz and took a day job at the New York Sports Club where he was a member. Between hanging out and working two jobs, he was barely getting any sleep, and his mom and I were concerned that he might fall asleep on his night job.

Sure enough, one night, he fell asleep and was given a warning, but it happened again, and they terminated him. He was so naive he couldn't believe his coworkers who he had asked to wake him up at the end of his break would allow him to oversleep and cause him to lose his job. Needless to say that one of those same coworkers has taken his job. Only working part-time at the gym, he couldn't afford to pay all his bills including his car note. So now I'm driving his Camaro, and there is not one day that I don't get some type of compliment about it when I'm in the Bronx or from some young buck who wants to race me on the parkway. Even kids as young as four are coming up to the car, pointing and saying, "You got a Camaro." Later, I found out from Larnelle that they have transformers for little kids that turn into Camaros. But with all its glare and glitter, it is only just a mode of transportation for me to get to and from work. Yet as painful as it may have seem at the time, I am thankful because things could've been worse. It took him a while as jobs are hard to come by these days, but thank God he is back on another job.

Learning to Let Go and Let God

A few years after taking my trip to Jamaica, I was feeling a little strapped for cash. It was during the Christmas season, and all the bills were pouring in, especially from my creditors who must've all conspired and decided that this was the perfect time of the year to charge me those high credit card renewal fees on top of the balance I already owed them. My kids were younger at the time, and I was feeling a little anxious about how the holidays were coming and not having enough money to pay my bills and buying them Christmas presents. I was faithfully paying 10 percent of my salary on tithe and offerings and wondered if God would mind if just this once, I borrowed the three hundred or so I used to give Him and spend it on my family. It was a real dilemma, and I was becoming very frustrated. I didn't know what to do and felt like giving up when a feeling inside directed me to let it go and trust God. At that very moment, a sudden calm came over me, and all my anxiety and frustration dissipated.

Sabbath came and I paid my tithes as usual, and I wasn't worrying about anything. I always paid my bills on Sundays, and that

Sunday when I began sorting through all my bills, I realized
I had received my monthly statement from my stockbroker. I
wasn't too excited because for months the stocks I had bought
were basically flat and weren't going up. I was tempted not to
open it for fear they were now in negative territory, and I had
lost money again. Trusting in God, I paid all my bills first and
then decided to open up the statement. I couldn't believe my
eyes. My stocks had gained value, and instead of a few hundred
dollars I thought I had, I was ten thousand dollars richer. Isn't
God good?

So this is what I have concluded from my trip to Jamaica and
the years following: that the spirit of God is within and with me,
urging me to let go so it can work for me, reminding me that it
has always been taking care of me, and will be with me forever
and for all eternity; that this physical body I am carrying around,
which is called David Heron is not who I really am; that my true
nature is spiritual and my physical state is an opportunity for me
to learn and to (definitely) remind other spiritual beings close
to me, having their own physical experiences, what life is really
about; that God's goodness is always present in and around us,
and all we have to do is to acknowledge and claim it through
faith; and that unhappiness is not part of God's plan for us but
a behavior we've learned and chosen to accept in our lives.

Do you ever remember seeing an unhappy baby? It wasn't until
we start to get older and saw other individuals demonstrating
unhappiness that we, as God's little children, begin to mimic
them and learn to display this behavior ourselves. Eventually, we
become so good at it. We also learn to become unhappy about
future events that have not even occurred yet. Still, if that's not
satisfying enough, some of us have to take it to the extreme by
making everyone around us unhappy. We do so by projecting
this behavior into unsuspecting others who unwittingly accept
it. After the choice has been made, there is enough unhappiness
to go around to make everyone feel unhappy. This has nothing

to do with sadness, which is an emotion that everyone feels from time to time.

Many of us have already discovered that happiness comes from within and that no one is responsible for our happiness. Just like unhappiness, there is a choice to be made, which isn't easy because unlearning a behavior we have been practicing all our lives can be difficult. After all, we can always find a million and one things from the past and the future to keep us in a state of perpetual unhappiness. Simply said, try to look at every situation you think will cause unhappiness as a challenge and that you have the ability within you to overcome every challenge. One day, I am going to write another book on this subject, but in the meantime, I strongly recommend reading *The Power of Now* by Eckhart Tolle. This book has done so much to help me grow as a person that I wish everyone would read it.

By the time this book has been published, I will have or will be in the process of downsizing. Both my wife and I have agreed that at this point and time in our lives less is more. We no longer need a death note, which is what a mortgage really is and have opted to get out of it and move into an apartment. We are going to stay home on our next vacation and get rid of all the stuff we've collected over the years that we thought we needed but have been really zapping us of our energy and live a simpler life. I will also be leaving my job at the Visiting Nurse Service of New York where I've been employed for the past ten years as a home-care nurse. Even though the decision was a little arduous, my transition from parole officer to nurse was not that difficult as I had always worked part-time as a nurse. I am grateful I was given this opportunity to work in a capacity where I could truly be of service to others.

It took a while, but after my trip to Jamaica and during the process of writing this book, I've come to realize that material possessions do not define who I am. The desire to have more and the need to be better off is no longer my goal in this life. I found that just being part of the human family and always doing the best I can is what it's all about. The truth is, no matter how important we think we are, we are all connected and are ultimately going to end up in the same position—without the status, the money, or the material possessions—when it's time to let go of this physical body. I pray that my children, whom I've been trying to convince there is more to life than the eyes can see, will embark upon the peace that awaits each one of us willing to let go of attachments. That would be remarkable.

Glossary of the Jamaican Dialect

a: To be, am, is, of, to, at,
brawta: A little extra
bruk: Break, broke
bumbo claat: Curse word
bwoy: boy
cutchie: Communal smoking pipe
dat: That
deh: Here, there
dem: Them
finga: Fingers
ginnal: A con artist
HIM: His Imperial Majesty referring to Haile Selassie I, former
    emperor of Ethiopia
irie: Good, nice, a salutation
Jah: God
Laad: Lord
likle: Little
litkle more: See you later
pon: On, upon
pickney: Child
puppa: Father
mi: I, me, mine
pum-pum: female sexual organ
Ras: Title given to Rastafarian as in Ras Ben, also means prince
rass or rass claat: Curse word

Rasta: Short for Rastafarian
seh: Say
spliff: Marijuana joint
yu or yuh: You
tief: Thief
wah: What
woklis: Worthless

Index